Central America

MANAGING EDITORS
Amy Bauman
Barbara J. Behm

CONTENT EDITORS
Amanda Barrickman
James I. Clark
Patricia Lantier
Charles P. Milne, Jr.
Katherine C. Noonan
Christine Snyder
Gary Turbak
William M. Vogt
Denise A. Wenger
Harold L. Willis
John Wolf

ASSISTANT EDITORS
Ann Angel
Michelle Dambeck
Barbara Murray
Renee Prink
Andrea J. Schneider

INDEXER
James I. Clark

ART/PRODUCTION
Suzanne Beck, Art Director
Andrew Rupniewski, Production Manager
Eileen Rickey, Typesetter

Library of Congress Number: 88-18337

2 3 4 5 6 7 8 9 0   97 96 95 94 93 92

Library of Congress Cataloging-in-Publication Data

Parisi, Vittorio.
  [America centrale. English]
  Central America / Vittorio Parisi.

  — (World nature encyclopedia)
  Translation of: America centrale.
  Includes index.
  Summary: Describes the natural and ecological niches,
boundaries, and life of the wildlife habitats of Central
America.
  1. Ecology—Central America—Juvenile literature.
2. Biotic communities—Central America—Juvenile
literature. [1. Ecology—Central America. 2. Biotic
communities—Central America.] I. Title. II. Series:
Nature nel mondo. English.
  QH108.A1P3713 1988 574.5′0972—dc19   88-18366
  ISBN 0-8172-3325-3

WORLD NATURE ENCYCLOPEDIA

Central America

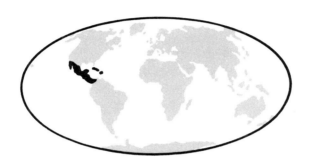

Vittorio Parisi

RAINTREE
STECK-VAUGHN
L I B R A R Y

Austin, Texas

CONTENTS

INTRODUCTION

Understanding the flora (plants), fauna (animals), and geology of Central America is difficult, even for a specialist.

Central America is many things, but above all it is a bridge, a connecting link between the vastly different continents of North and South America. The region's flora and fauna had a complex origin and are still the object of many scientific studies today. It is exciting to study the events which brought the plants and animals to this area.

About 130 million years ago, South America stood as a virtual island. Its animals included marsupials (mammals that carry their young in a pouch), the ancestors of modern day sloths, armadillos, and anteaters. It also was home to extremely large herbivores (plant-eating animals). For example, the giant three-toed sloth, which had a long neck and a short trunk similar to that of a tapir, grew to 16 feet (5

meters) in length. There also was an armored mammal similar to an armadillo that was as large as a rhinoceros. Later, to the north, the continent now called North America separated from the huge land mass that also included Europe and Asia. Here, mammals were the dominant fauna, including various types of dogs, cats, and rodents. Surprisingly, monkeys also populated parts of North America.

The fauna of this region is thought to have been more changeable than that of South America. In part, this was because new animals were continually migrating to North America from Asia across the frozen Bering Strait.

For millions of years, North and South America remained separated. On each continent, the plants and animals grew and evolved in complete isolation from those in the other region.

THE ORIGIN OF CENTRAL AMERICA

About twenty million years ago, the huge plates that form the earth's crust began to change position. The plate under the Pacific Ocean moved eastward, and its leading edge was forced under the plate that lay at the bottom of the Caribbean Sea. As the moving rock sank deeper into the earth, it melted, came under pressure, and finally surged upward to form a series of volcanoes.

The tips of these underwater mountains now protruded from the sea where before there had been no dry land. Like a chain, they loosely connected the vast land masses that lay to the north and the south.

As the geologic process of shifting plates continued, more and more solid ground emerged from the sea. Finally, during the Pliocene epoch (two million to twelve million years ago), the action was largely complete. A continuous line of mountains now connected the two great land masses. Central America had been born. A bridge now existed between North and South America.

Immediately, plants and animals began to colonize this new land. North American species of plants and animals began to move south toward the warm, humid environment. Southern species began to move north, especially along the coasts.

Biologically, Central America became an area of transition between a stable South America and a dynamic North America. Later, of course, the distribution of plants and animals in Central America was greatly affected by glacial periods and by the actions of humans.

Neither the Isthmus of Tehuantepec nor the Isthmus of Panama was or is an obstacle for any South American species migrating northward. Still, the farther north the area, the fewer animals of South American origin that can be seen. For example, hummingbirds and morpho butterflies become increasingly rare in northern Mexico as the evergreen and rain forest areas diminish.

Incidentally, morpho butterflies are magnificent insects with beautiful wings that feature metallic reflections. They originated in the basins of the Amazon and Orinoco rivers. They are closely associated with tropical forests and are unable to cross even small stretches of sea. As a result, they are not found at all in the Antilles islands.

Other species present in Central America have a definite northern origin. Bears, felines (catlike animals), canines (doglike animals), some groups of rodents, camel-like animals, certain bats, tapirs, wild goats, pronghorn antelope,

Preceding pages: Shown is a view of the ruins of the Aztec city of Uzmal in the Yucatan forest.

Opposite page: The mouth of the crater of Popocatepetl Volcano in central Mexico is pictured. The varied and colorful Central American landscape includes mountains covered with pines, desert plateaus, flatlands, and mountain ranges covered with dense tropical forests.

The formation of the Isthmus of Panama with the connection of North and South America is a relatively recent geological episode. It dates back only a few million years. Before then, the animal species of the two continents had evolved independently of each other. They had virtually nothing in common. After the formation of the isthmus, however, a rapid migration began. The two different faunas came into contact, and the northern species (pumas, tapirs, and guanacos, which are related to the camel family) began their spectacular invasion of South America. The movement of animals from South America to North America was less extraordinary. Many of the ancient South American species were not able to withstand the competition of the new northern predators. Therefore, they quickly became extinct. Finally, in other cases, the North American species survived only in the territories they conquered. Such is the case with tapirs and guanacos.

and piglike animals all have North American or Eurasian origins. They moved toward South America in various migrations.

During the formation of the Isthmus of Panama, these animals "invaded" South America either along the Andes or by fanning out across the wide eastern plains. In their migrations, they eliminated many native tropical species that were less competitive.

Typical tropical species found in Central America include various toothless mammals (edentate), marsupials, and rodents such as pacas which are large, white-spotted, and almost tailless. Others are the agoutis rodents, various bats, hummingbirds, tinamous, and other birds. In addition, there are many insect species that are typically tropical, including the stingless bees.

In general, as they moved north, none of these animals went very far beyond the Isthmus of Panama and never progressed far into North America. This generalization, however, has a few notable exceptions. The nine-banded armadillo and the Virginia opossum, two of the most com-

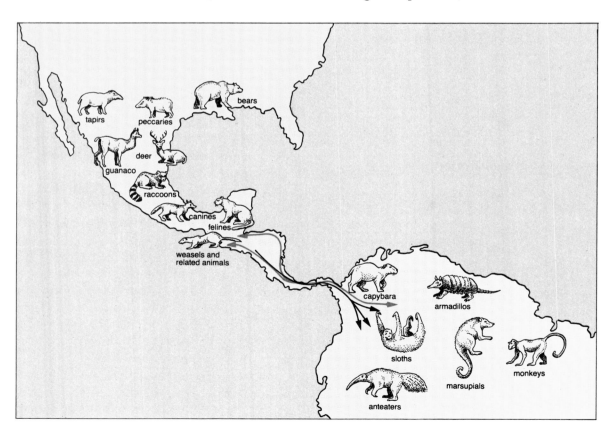

The ability of different animal groups to colonize new geographic areas depends on their ability to adapt and on the continuity and stability of their new habitat. If crucial habitat is destroyed, they may be unable to spread through disconnected zones. If enough habitat is lost, the animals may disappear entirely. A good example of this is the morpho butterfly. Originally from the forests of the Amazon Basin, these butterflies were able to reach Central America by moving across the forest habitat, which at one time was continuous. However, they were never able to reach the Antilles.

Following pages: A desolate view of the calanchi, the most arid region of the plateaus of Mexico, is seen.

mon mammals in the United States, have South American origins.

Once they were established in Central America, the plants and animals that had come from North and South America evolved into new forms. These forms today make this region different from any other part of the world.

Mexico: Almost a Subcontinent

By far the most dominating presence in Central America is that of Mexico. Mexico lies mostly in Central America and is of great importance in the history of American civilization. Humans first arrived in this region more than 25,000 years ago, long after the geologic events that created the flora and fauna had already taken place. Some ancient civilizations, such as the Mayas and the Aztecs, developed extremely high levels of culture and technology. Surprisingly, these advanced people began as a primitive culture of mastodon hunters. (Mastodons were huge elephant-like animals.) Evidence of their primitive ancestors was found years ago in excavations at Santa Isabel Iztapan.

Mexico has since become a melting pot of people. After the Spanish conquest, Mexico became the scene of many never-ending battles. Important environmental changes here are still linked to increasing industrialization and to the phenomenon of urban sprawl. However, large natural areas do continue to exist, both in the arid northern part of the country and in the humid forests of Yucatán and Chiapas.

The vast area of Mexico and the West Indies extends approximately from 32 degrees to 10 degrees north latitude. Going from east to west, the land mass is narrower. This area can be divided into three parts—North-Central Mexico, Southern Mexico, and the Caribbean zone.

The flora and fauna of North America predominate from the interior regions of Mexico to the Continental Divide, the Volcanic Sierra Dividing Line. On the Atlantic and Pacific coasts, however, there exist neotropical plants and animals that are of South American origin. Neotropical refers to the region stretching southward from the Tropic of Cancer and including southern Mexico, Central America, South America, and the West Indies.

Extending over an area of 762,032 square miles (1,973,663 square kilometers), Mexico has a surprising variety of environments. They include dry and inhospitable desert areas, southern rain forests, and the barren sierras (mountain ranges) of the north-central region.

The northern region of Mexico is divided into sections stretching from the Pacific Ocean to the Atlantic Ocean in a north-south direction. They are: the Lower California peninsula, the western coastal plains, the Sierra Madre Occidental, the southern plains, the Sierra Madre Oriental, and the coastal plains of the Gulf of Mexico. Some of these sections extend rather deeply into the south. The Sierra Madre Occidental, for example, reaches as far as the Continental Divide.

The high central plains, the heart of the country, extend from the western mountain chain to the Sierra Madre Occidental.

The zone south of the Continental Divide is extremely complicated. Traditionally, the following regions are recognized: the great depression of Balsas, carved out by the river of the same name; the Oaxaclan-Pueblo mountain range; the Papaloapán plains; and the southern Sierra Madre mountains. Then there are the plains of the Isthmus of Tehuantepec, which separate the main part of Mexico from two other large regions which are the Yucatán and the

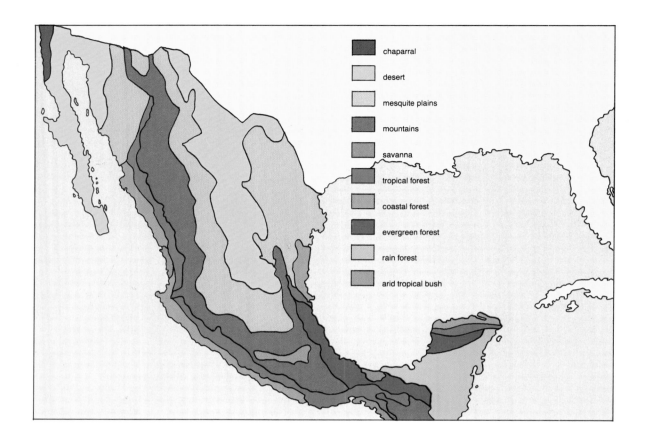

The legend reads:

- chaparral
- desert
- mesquite plains
- mountains
- savanna
- tropical forest
- coastal forest
- evergreen forest
- rain forest
- arid tropical bush

The presence of the sierras in the interior of Mexico causes the climatic and vegetation zones of Central America to have a northwest-southeast orientation. This is different from the more common latitudinal north-south bands that are found on the African continent. The different types of vegetation include greatly-contrasting forests (from the conifer forests of the mountains to the tropical rain forests), numerous varieties of shrub areas, subdesert, and arid zones. The arid landscapes are perhaps the most common images foreigners have of the country of Mexico.

territory of the Chiapas including the Sierra Madre del Chiapas and the plains.

From a climatic point of view, Mexico can be divided into four large regions (which were already partially known in the period following the European discovery of the area). These include the arid zone (about 52 percent of the country), which includes the area up to the California Peninsula and most of the northern region with the exception of the plains of the Gulf of Mexico; the semiarid zone (about 31 percent of the country), which makes up the central part of the nation with a wide stretch toward the south; the semi-humid zone (about 10 percent of the country), which, except for a small area on the Pacific Ocean (the Tepic territory) is located entirely along the Atlantic Ocean from Tampico south; the humid zone (about 7 percent of the country), an area of limestone soils largely covered by rain forests at the base of the Yucatán.

The most important points to remember about these zones are that most of Mexico is arid or semiarid, and the

Pictured is a ranch in the region of Chiapas, Mexico. Numerous edible plants were native to Central America when the Spanish conqueror Cortés invaded. Many were already known and used by the Aztecs. Maize, or corn, existed in a cultivated form that was a descendant of teosinte, a tall grassy plant found in Mexico. The natives often used tomatoes and peppers for sauces. They made tasty beverages with cocoa. The true potato is South American, not Central American, in origin, but the Aztecs used other tuberous plants that were closely related to the potato.

areas of highest rainfall are found near the Atlantic Ocean or in the southern part of the country.

To a great extent, the Mexican vegetation areas overlap the climatic zones mentioned above. From west to east and from north to south, various groups are found. These include desert vegetation; the chaparral of the Lower California peninsula; forests of acacias and tree cacti; forests of pines and oaks of the sierras together with the northern vegetation of the mountain peaks; tropical evergreen forests and rain forests; and, at higher elevations, the cloud forests.

This breakdown does not take into account the extreme diversification and richness of the Mexican vegetation. More than three hundred types of oaks, six hundred species of orchids, and more than half of the world's species of cacti exist in Mexico.

With so many species of plants, it is easy to understand why botany is an ancient science in Mexico. The famous plant collection of Montezuma was perhaps the first botanic garden in the world. The Aztecs actually used more than three thousand species of plants for medicinal purposes.

The origin of the Mexican flora is as complex as the origin of its fauna.

THE PLATEAU AND SIERRA ENVIRONMENTS

Very rich flora and fauna make up the complex environmental mosaic of the plateaus and sierras. A series of different life forms is found from the arid northern territory to the rain forest of Chiapas. Their distribution pattern results from the complex history of the development of the plant and animal communities in the large Central American territory.

The scenery of northern Mexico has been described many times in western movies, advertising, and books. In the midday heat of an adobe Indian village called a "pueblo," people sleep through the "siesta," the afternoon nap. Arid environments with tall, columnar cacti can be seen alongside meager cultivations of beans, which is practically the national dish of Mexico. These are scattered around expanses of mesquite shrubs, with acacias and other parched plants growing around the village.

This is the landscape of a large part of Mexico, from the border with the United States to the Continental Divide. This landscape, which extends even to the highlands, surrounds a traveler for miles and miles. The arid zone is not limited to the northern plains but also reaches into the high central plains and other areas. In some places, the extreme dryness has created rather large desert areas, such as the Altar Desert in the state of Sonora and the Balsas Depression farther south.

The vegetation of the arid environments is dominated by cacti. These include the giant columnar cacti of the *Cereus* genus, different species of mammillary cacti with well-marked leaf cushions, and prickly pears.

Other plants typical of dry environments are yuccas, mesquites, and century plants. *Agave atrovierns* and *Agave tequilana*, from which the alcoholic beverages pulque and tequila are made, grow here. In some places where conditions are less severe, bushes and some trees are found growing along with the grasses.

The desolate look of the arid zones changes dramatically after the rains, which are rare but torrential. When the rain comes, there is a virtual explosion of lush vegetation that had been dormant. Suddenly the desert is transformed into a blooming blaze of colors, and the air is perfumed with the aroma of flowers. Just as quickly, however, the lush vegetation dries up and disappears. The plants return to a dormant state, which enables them to survive the intense heat.

This environment is rather poor in resources and is

Opposite page: Shown is a view of the Sierra Madre Occidental with vegetation typical of arid zones. This type of environment dominates a good part of the Mexican landscape on the plains, the plateaus, and the sierras.

characterized by limited ecological diversity. The starkness fades away, however, as the elevation rises along the sierras. This is especially true in regions with large volcanic mountains. Here, the environment becomes richer with vegetation, and at an altitude of over 8,202 feet (2,500 m), lush pine and oak forests appear. At even higher elevations these gradually give way to spruce and fir forests.

The flora of Mexico includes no fewer than eight different kinds of conifer trees, with a total of seventy-two species. There are at least twenty-eight species of pines and many more forms and varieties. There are also abundant species of firs, spruces, cypresses, and junipers. These conifer forests are home to a rich and varied fauna. The animals easily find refuge and food in the trees, which are often hundreds of years old. But it is not only the forests of the sierras that are a refuge to the great variety of animals of Central America. Many Central American species can be found in other environments of the region as well. Some of these animals now live in harmony with humans and have adapted well to the partially urbanized areas.

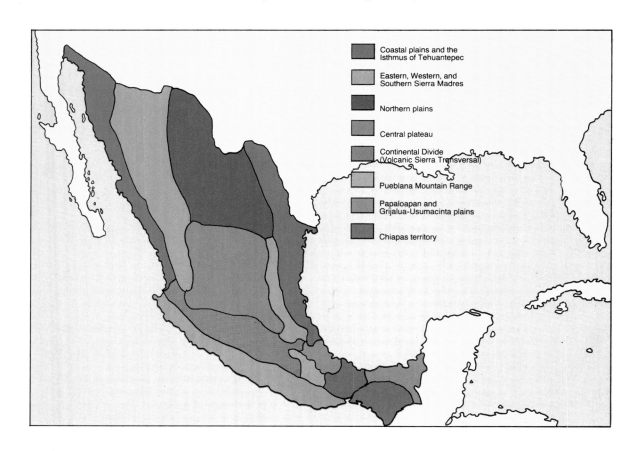

Coastal plains and the Isthmus of Tehuantepec

Eastern, Western, and Southern Sierra Madres

Northern plains

Central plateau

Continental Divide (Volcanic Sierra Transversal)

Pueblana Mountain Range

Papaloapan and Grijalua-Usumacinta plains

Chiapas territory

Carnivores

The coyote is perhaps the animal best suited for life in the plateau and sierra environments. The coyote is a canine (dog family) like the wolf and fox. All three belong to the genus *Canis*. The coyote is extremely capable of adapting to various environmental conditions, and it is also very good at resisting the intrusion of humans into its territory.

In the local language, this animal is called the "coyotl," and earlier peoples also referred to it as the "coyocan" and "coyotopec." It lives throughout much of Mexico, even in dense southern forests in such places as the Yucatan Peninsula. The coyote stands about 20 inches (50 centimeters) tall at the shoulder and is about 3 feet (1 m) long. Its bushy tail is about 16 inches (40 cm) long.

The coyote is lean and fast. It hunts small animals, especially rodents, but will also eat insects, carrion (dead animals), and garbage. It is not afraid to prey upon livestock on ranches or upon pets in city suburbs. It is an especially adaptable animal that knows exactly how to make use of any available food source. In fact, the coyote owes its widespread existence to this very skill.

Most coyotes, however, live away from people—either alone in a solitary life-style or in a monogamous (having

The coyote, a canine whose size is between that of a wolf and a fox, resembles the fox more than the wolf because of its ability to adapt to every type of environment and food source. Despite many years of ruthless persecution, the coyote shows no signs of diminishing in numbers. Nor does it appear to be leaving the areas where its survival would seem to be more difficult.

19

big-eared fox

spotted skunk

common striped skunk

cacomistle

only one mate) relationship with another coyote. Though it is unusual, coyotes have been known to run in packs like wolves in their constant search for food.

Other native canine species also live in Mexico. Perhaps the most famous of these is the wolf, called "lobo." The Mexican wolf belongs to the same species as the North American timber wolf, but it is a different variety or race. In Mexico, wolves range to the western edge of the Sierra Madre Mountains, which is the southern extreme of the timber wolf's distribution. Wolves are quickly becoming very rare in Mexico.

The big-eared fox resembles the African desert fox. It is a small carnivore (meat-eater) that lives in the arid regions of the Lower California peninsula. It can be found as far into the Mexican interior as Chihuahua and Coahuila.

Another canine that can be found quite easily throughout the entire territory is the gray fox, which originated in temperate North America.

This species exists even in the northernmost part of South America. It is, therefore, a good example of a species that was able to cross the Isthmus of Panama as it spread southward. The gray fox is about 1.5 feet (45 cm) long, stands 1 foot (30 cm) tall at the shoulders, and has a tail that measures about 16 inches (40 cm). Its back is silver-gray with streaks of black, and its belly is covered with white fur bordered by yellow.

The Mexican fox is an efficient predator of rodents and other creatures, including small birds and insects. It also eats some plants. For example, if it is hunting for rodents near a cornfield, it may well eat a few ears of corn in addition to the prey it catches. It is not afraid to approach human habitation in its search for food. This very adaptable species is an important member of the food chain in many parts of Mexico.

The American badger is an animal similar to the European badger, although the American version is a bit stockier. It typically measures less than 3 feet (1 m) in length and has a tail that is no longer than 6 inches (15 cm). A distinguishing characteristic of this animal is a white stripe that runs from its nose to its rear. The badger prefers to live in a dry environment that has some bushes and trees.

The local people call this mustelid (which is an animal belonging to the weasel family) the *tlalcoyote*, which means "ground coyote." This is a clear and not surprising reference to this animal's ability to live under the ground.

An albino skunk in captivity is pictured. This type of skunk was quickly domesticated in America just as it was in Europe. It is considered a delightful pet. The horrible odor that is typical of these animals is sprayed only in defense. Under normal circumstances, domestic skunks do not use this defense. Nevertheless, pet skunk owners often have the anal glands that secrete the odor removed when the skunks are very young.

The badger is indeed a very strong digger, and it uses this skill to capture rodents and insects by destroying their dens and capturing them underground.

Mexico has three species of skunks—the striped skunk, the spotted skunk, and the hog-nosed skunk. The latter is often completely black except for a white spot on its nose.

The best-known skunk is the striped, locally called the "zorillo listado." It is rather widespread in Mexico, living in both mountainous and desert areas. It is, however, not easy to observe because it leads a nocturnal life searching for prey in the grass and brush at night. Its body, which is about 16 inches (40 cm) long, has the characteristic skunk coloration of black and white stripes.

When alarmed by the presence of a potential enemy, the skunk makes a circular series of little jumps to warn the attacker. If that technique doesn't work, the skunk points its rear toward the other animal and raises its long, bushy tail. This is an indication that the skunk is about to spray the attacker with the terrible-smelling liquid stored in its glands. The foul spray is a defense mechanism that drives the skunk's enemies away.

Shown is a field of century plants on the Mexican plateaus. Mexicans make their potent drink tequila with the fermented juice of this plant.

Below: A puma runs through in a grassland area. Originally from North America, this large, magnificent cat spread southward, populating all of South America over the last million years. The puma resembles the African lion because of its adaptation to hot, arid, rocky regions and because of its uniformly-colored coat. Its nickname is "mountain lion."

Opposite page: The hind part of the pronghorn is white and covered with straight hair. It functions as an "alarm" for the rest of the herd. When the pronghorn sees danger, these tail hairs stand on end, reflect the sunlight, and are visible for quite a distance.

Another common carnivore in Mexico is the cacomistle, which is a member of the same animal family as the raccoon. The cacomistle has a head like a cat, large eyes, well-developed and hairless ears, and measures less than 3 feet (1 m) in length. As a timid, nocturnal animal, it can be very difficult to observe. Mostly, the cacomistle eats rodents, but it is also a good tree climber and has been known to prey on birds in trees. When it climbs, its ringed tail often remains perfectly straight.

Both brown and grizzly bears have survived in northern Mexico, especially in the area around Chihuahua. They are found most often in mountainous and hilly regions that have a minimal forest covering. These bears rarely exist in Mexico's arid zones.

Mexico also has a widespread population of pumas. Sometimes called the mountain lion or cougar, the puma is an excellent example of a northern species that spread south into South America after the formation of the Isthmus of Panama.

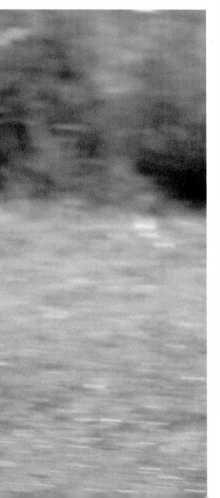

Today, the puma can be found from Canada to Patagonia, and in some places it is heavily hunted by humans. Though superbly adapted to the arid, rocky environment of the mountains and hills, this cat is also at home in the forest. Normally, the puma preys upon deer, but it is also adept at taking smaller animals.

The puma is about 4 feet (130 cm) long and stands 30 inches (75 cm) tall at the shoulders. Its thick tail adds another 28 inches (70 cm) to its length. Depending upon the area in which the puma lives, the color of its fur may range from dark brown to reddish yellow. Normally, it is tan or light gray. The puma's belly is generally covered with lighter colored fur, and its tail is tipped with black.

Another feline present in Mexico is the bobcat. This cat, which is much smaller than the puma, can be identified by its short, stubby tail. Although it is quite rare, this cat does exist in some mountainous portions of Mexico that have sparse tree cover. Farther north in the United States and parts of Canada, this animal is rather common.

Known locally as the "borrego," the bighorn sheep stands about 3 feet (1 m) tall at the shoulders and sports a pair of large, curving horns similar to those of the mouflon, a wild sheep found in Europe. Although they are grazers, bighorns often live in rugged terrain, not far from the safety of rocky cliffs. During much of the year, they live in sexually-segregated herds. In Mexico, bighorn sheep live primarily in the mountainous regions of the Lower California peninsula. During the annual mating season, bighorn rams (males) battle for breeding rights to the females. They do this by charging each other at high speed and banging their heads together. Sometimes this sound can be heard for great distances in the quiet mountain air. Though the collisions are quite violent, the rams' skulls are equipped to withstand such blows, and serious injuries are rare.

Bighorn sheep also live or formerly lived throughout much of North America and eastern Siberia, two places that are now separated by the Bering Strait. The sheep's presence on both sides of the strait is one more proof that some species of flora and fauna came to the Americas from Asia.

The pronghorn antelope is a hoofed animal that stands about 32 inches (80 cm) high at the shoulders and can be found in the northernmost part of the Lower California peninsula and in the Mexican states of Sonora, Chihuahua, and Coahuila. Pronghorns are thought to be the descendants of an ancient group of animals that once inhabited the Americas. In 1800, there were approximately forty million of these animals in North America. Although the population declined dramatically for a time, pronghorn numbers have recently increased significantly.

The animal's name comes from the point, or prong, found near the tip of its horns. Unlike many horned animals which regularly shed their antlers, the pronghorn maintains a permanent base for its horns. The horn's outside sheath is replaced annually, but the core remains.

Pronghorn antelope generally live in small groups composed of one male, called a "buck," and a harem of three to eight females, called "does." Pronghorns have excellent eyesight and are among the fastest land animals in the world. Members of a herd communicate via chemical signals that come from glands located beneath the ears, at the base of the tail, behind the heel, and between the two parts of the hoof. They also can signal danger by causing the white hair on their rumps to stand up straight.

Two species of "peccary," the American equivalent of the European wild boar, are found in Mexico. These are the collared peccary and the white-lipped peccary. Although it prefers areas protected by trees, the collared peccary is found throughout Mexico. The white-lipped variety is more numerous in the south and is closely associated with the forest.

The collared peccary is about 3 feet (1 m) long, has a shoulder height of perhaps 24 inches (62 cm), and weighs up to 60 pounds (27 kilogram). It is an omnivore, meaning it eats both plants and animals. Packs of peccaries, containing as many as thirty animals, are constantly on the move in search of food.

Various species of hares are present on the Mexican plains. Generally, they are northern animals that have spread south, but some native species are also present. One worth mentioning is the volcano rabbit, which is found in the high elevation regions of Popocatepetl and Iztaccíhuatl.

Both North and South America are populated by numerous species of rodents found nowhere else in the world. Many of these exist in great numbers, indicating that they have adapted very successfully to their environment. Among the most common of these are deer mice, which are similar to European mice, and exist on both the low and high plains. Ground squirrels and prairie dogs are also found in northern Mexico.

Another Mexican rodent is the kangaroo rat, an amaz-

Opposite page: The cactus wren, which can be as big as a lark, is one of the largest birds of its family. This bird is easily recognizable because of its shape, its characteristic movements, its striped plumage, and its preference for arid habitat. The cactus wren's song is made up of a series of low, monotonous notes and is one of the most familiar sounds of the American deserts.

Some of the characteristic birds of the Mexican high plains are *from left to right, and from top to bottom:* the red-backed migrating thrush, the curved-beak mockingbird, the wild turkey, and the dark towhee are found in the more dense chaparral areas and in some open forests. The turkey vulture (in flight) is found in all environments. Other birds in the picture include a family of quail, a characteristic bird of the more arid regions; the common mockingbird (with its wings spread); the mourning dove (in flight); and the troupial, a species typical of the regions having denser vegetation.

ing animal that has adapted exceedingly well to life in an arid environment. This animal is able to survive in extremely dry areas by utilizing the moisture contained in the vegetable matter it eats.

Pack rats are also particularly well adapted to dry environments. As their name suggests, these animals have the odd habit of accumulating all kinds of objects in their nests. They especially seem to like sparkling items, including bits of glass and aluminum foil.

Birds

From an ornithological point of view, the Mexican Sierra territory can be divided into three areas. The northern part is the largest, but has the fewest bird species. The central part has its best bird habitat in the areas of the Continental Divide and the Sierra Madres. The southern part is the smallest, but it has the most abundant bird life, primarily because of its humid climate. From the north, an arid wedge penetrates into Mexico as far as the Isthmus of Tehuantepec. At this point, the dry climate becomes more moist, and tropical species of birds begin to appear.

Following pages: The black buzzard is a large predator of small animals such as toads, crabs, and freshwater crayfish. It is typical of the areas covered with trees not far from water, especially in the coastal regions of the Gulf of California and the Caribbean Sea. When flying, the tail and wings of this bird appear larger than those of a normal buzzard. Its yellow legs and talons, two white spots on its wings, and the white of its tail stand out against its black feathers. The young of this species, however, are light in color and can be identified only by their silhouette.

It seems apparent that the dry climate of the interior has prevented the tropical species from spreading north. This area, with its moderate climate, also serves as the wintering ground for many bird species that spend the warm season farther north. Some species, in fact, travel great distances in annual migrations between this region and Alaska and Canada far to the north.

The arid wedge itself is characterized by a desert or semidesert environment that has been colonized by cacti, agaves (fleshy-leaved plants), and some hardy species of grasses. Often, these areas blend into zones where dry bushes and frail mesquite shrubs are found.

Some typical North American species such as the mockingbird, mourning dove, and turkey vulture are commonly found in these areas. Also existing here are southern species like the cactus wren, white-necked crow, and Inca dove. Many of these are found in the southwestern part of the United States as well.

An interesting example of the local bird life is the curved-beak mockingbird, which nests in mesquite shrubs and thistles.

As they do elsewhere in the world, some bird species in Mexico are attracted to centers of human habitation by the increased supplies of cover and food. Naturally, these birds must be able to tolerate the unique conditions that human presence creates. Some of these birds, like the house sparrow, are the same ones that are attracted to humans around the world. Others are native species, such as the Mexican house finch and the Inca dove.

In large cities, bird life often centers on the wooded parks that humans have created. These areas are good places to observe birds, especially since many of the species that live there are not particularly afraid of humans. Besides the song sparrow and Inca dove, which are often seen in squares and streets, birds like troupials and the migrating thrush are also found there. All of these city-dwelling birds have a northern origin. Of the seventeen species recognized by ornithologists, only two are not found in the United States. All of the species in the nearby archaeological area of Teotihuacan are also North American.

By contrast, in the spruce and fir forests of the Desierto de los Leones, at least nine of nineteen species are not found in the United States. The pine forests of the Sierra Madres, therefore, represent a peculiar habitat that has attracted a unique type of bird life with different native species.

A rich, diversified bird population occurs in this area because of the high humidity and abundant food. Of the thirty-three species easily observed here, fourteen are found only in Mexico.

Fir and spruce forests also occur at higher elevations, thereby providing a habitat for other species. Among those characteristic of this kind of environment are cactus wrens and trogons, 12-inch (30 cm) birds with a green and blue back, yellow belly with a white stripe, and gray head, neck, and breast. Trogons are typically tropical birds, but one species, the coppery-tailed trogon, lives as far north as New Mexico and Texas.

A bird that is widely distributed throughout this type of environment is the golden-crowned kinglet, a grayish bird with a yellow or reddish patch on the crown of its head. Another common species is the crested flycatcher. This bird is included among Central and South American species, although it actually belongs to the tyrant flycatcher or the American flycatcher family that is more widespread in the northern part of the continent.

Another characteristic group of birds is the humming-

A very young iguana is pictured. Other species of iguanas in Mexico include small anole lizards and large black iguanas, or false iguanas, which are characteristic of Central America.

birds, of which there are at least thirty species in the Mexican Sierra Madres. Hummingbirds are the smallest birds in the world. They exist from Canada to Argentina, but most species are located in the tropical zones. All hummingbirds have long, thin beaks, which they use to collect nectar from flowers. They suspend themselves in midair by beating their wings as rapidly as twenty-nine times per second.

In Mexico, the most important of these are the green, violet-eared hummingbirds and the white-eared hummingbirds. The latter are found primarily in the mountains, while

the former are more tropical birds. A third species, the magnificent hummingbird, is also commonly found in the mountains. With a length of about 5 inches (13 cm), this bird is larger than the other two. It has a green back, a purple crown on its head, and a metallic green throat.

The parrot family is also well represented in Central America. Eighteen parrot species exist in Mexico, mostly in the sierra zones. The most famous and spectacular of these birds is the military macaw, which inhabits conifer and mixed forests. The macaw, which measures about 28 inches (70 cm) in length, is most commonly found in the area of Durango.

Another well-known parrot is the large-beaked parrot, which is about 15 inches (38 cm) long. This bird sports intense green plumage with red shoulders and front. It is found in conifer forests of the Sierra Madre Occidental as far as the high central plains of Michoacan.

Many woodpeckers and other birds are also found in this region. Included among these are both diurnal (active during the day) and nocturnal birds of prey.

Wild turkeys can be found in forest clearings that have abundant food sources. Farmyard turkeys around the world descended from this large wild bird, which was domesticated in ancient Mexico and other places. In the wild, they live in small groups, each of which is composed of several females and one male.

Reptiles

The high, arid areas of the Mexican plateaus are populated by numerous species of reptiles. Most of these are lizards and snakes, although there are some turtles.

Lizards, including the iguana family, have a wide variety of forms and adaptations. Proof of this fact can be seen in the agile little anole lizards. More than three hundred species of anole lizards are distributed throughout Central and South America and the West Indies. These include spiny lizards, which sport rough, backward-pointing scales. Further examples can be found in the genus *Phrynosoma* and in the horned toad family. Horned toads look like miniature dinosaurs, with sharp spikes and spines. Gila monsters constitute another group of unique lizards. These animals are notorious because they are one of the few remaining poisonous lizards. Because their bites can be fatal, gila monsters pose a significant threat to humans.

There are only two species in the gila monster family,

Rattlesnakes are predators of warm-blooded animals. These snakes have specialized heat-sensitive organs that enable them to sense even at a distance the body temperature of potential prey. The crackling sound of a snake's rattle is a threat for many species, and they quickly run away when they hear it. This technique is copied by other animals to drive away predators that mistake the sound for a rattlesnake. Young owls *(bottom illustration)*, threatened by a coyote, emit a sound similar to a rattle from their nest, which immediately drives the coyote away.

and both are found in Mexico. They are the gila monster and the beaded lizard. The gila monster is larger, 24 to 30 inches (60 to 75 cm) and is concentrated in the north, primarily in the state of Sonora. It can be identified by its yellow spots. The small, beaded lizard is about 20 inches (50 cm) long and is more widely distributed throughout Mexico, but it is most often found in the west. It too, has spots, but they are usually orange or red.

These stocky reptiles with fat tails live primarily in arid desert regions. During times of extreme heat, they seek refuge in underground dens that they or other animals have dug. The female typically lays three to thirteen eggs, and the young hatch in about a month. At birth, they are already about 8 inches (20 cm) long.

Usually, gila monsters hunt at night, preying mostly on other reptiles or their eggs, and small rodents and birds. They hold their prey still with their powerful jaws, while poisonous teeth slowly inject poison into the victim. When hunting is poor, gila monsters are able to survive long periods without food because of the fat deposits in their tails. The mountains are home to many species of poisonous and nonpoisonous snakes. With two exceptions, the nonpoisonous varieties all belong to the colubrid family, and the poisonous ones to the pit viper family. The exceptions are the magnificent coral snakes and the mambas, which are members of the elapid family.

Copperheads and water moccasins are pit vipers, but probably the most famous members of that family are the rattlesnakes. Most of the world's twenty-five species of rattlesnakes are found in Mexico and the southern United States. They range in size from about 20 inches (50 cm) to 6.5 feet (2 m).

Among the better-known species of "rattlers" are the diamondback and western rattlesnakes, both common in the southern United States and Mexico. Another is the South American rattlesnake which, as its name implies, has spread farther south. There is also the pygmy rattlesnake, which can be found on Mexican plateaus. A rattlesnake's chief identifying feature, of course, is the rattle at the end of its tail. Typically, the rattle is made up of about ten horny rings that produce a characteristic sound when shaken. Not all pit vipers have rattles, however. Three pit vipers that do not have them are water moccasins, copperheads, and the fer-de-lance, a widespread species of rather large snakes.

Some zoologists have a theory that rattlesnakes evolved

The eastern diamondback rattlesnake is one of the most widespread rattlers in the arid regions of North and Central America. Somewhat similar to the vipers of the Old World, these reptiles are distinguished by their heat-sensitive organs that appear as dimples between the nose and the eyes. The rattle, which is not present in all pit viper snakes (the family to which rattlesnakes belong), is located at the end of its body. It is made of a series of horny rings that are formed at the end of the tail every time the rattler sheds its skin (more than once a year).

their rattles long ago when huge herds of grazing animals such as bison, deer, and antelope covered the prairies of North and Central America. The rattle may have been a way for a snake to signal its presence.

The Spadefoot Toad

Frogs and toads are especially well suited for life in dry climates.

Perhaps the best example of this is an adaptable animal called the spadefoot toad. The spadefoot has learned to survive long periods of drought by retreating

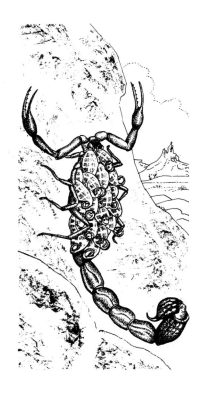

deep inside holes dug in the ground. In fact, it comes out of the ground only when the humidity is high enough to sustain its life processes. Usually, this occurs only after a steady rain.

The Invertebrates

Invertebrates are animals that do not have backbones. Included among these in Mexico are a variety of scorpions, snails, spiders, and insects. The scorpion is one well-known invertebrate that has made the necessary adaptations for life in an arid environment. The scorpion is thought to be one of the oldest land inhabitants on earth.

Many insects also live in the arid areas of Mexico. Among these are darkling beetles, dung beetles, and beautiful butterflies that live even in areas with only slight vegetative cover. There are also numerous species of spiders living primarily under the ground and in shrubs. Some are noted for their brilliant colors and huge spines.

Because of Mexico's warm climate, many animals migrate there in the winter from North America. These include vertebrate animals such as birds and bats, but some

Scorpions, acclaimed for their dangerous stings, are interesting animals with a very ancient origin. Their first fossil remains date from the Silurian period, five million years ago. They are highly evolved in their sexual behavior, which is characterized by a complex dance that precedes mating. They are also highly evolved in parental care. The young, as the illustration shows, climb on the back of the mother as soon as they are born. They remain under her protection until their exoskeletons, or external shells, have hardened enough to make them less vulnerable.

The splendid monarch butterfly is one of the most famous migratory invertebrates. On the opposite page, the map of Central and North America shows their summer (black circles) and winter (red circles) habitats. As the map illustrates, they generally tend to move southeast in the fall and northwest in the spring. Much of the eastern North American monarch population spends the winter in the cold conifer forests of the Mexican mountains. Here, at about fifty locations situated around nineteen degrees north latitude, they gather in great concentrations.

insects also make the long journey. Chief among these is the brightly-colored monarch butterfly. This large insect has red or orange wings bordered in black with a yellowish underside.

During the spring and summer, monarchs live and re-produce throughout much of the United States. Each winter, however, they migrate south to spend the winter in Mexico. They always go to the same places on the Lower California peninsula and in the state of Michoacan. These places are generally covered with shrubs and may be as high as 9,843 feet (3,000 m). Huge numbers of butterflies may be involved in the migration. Once, scientists estimated that fourteen million butterflies wintered on only 4 acres (1.5 hectares.).

Mexico also has many gastropods, which are snails that live in humid forests at high elevations. But because of the abundance of limestone in arid regions, they can also live in a dry environment. Those that live in dry areas survive by burrowing beneath the limestone soil. One kind of snail has an unusual spiral shell. Another has small teeth to help protect it from bats and other predators.

SUBTERRANEAN LIFE

Mexico has many caves. Often, they are part of extensive, complex subterranean or underground limestone systems. Hundreds of these caves have been found in the states of Yucatán, Veracruz, Tamaulipas, San Luis Potosi, Morelos, and Guerrero. Many are very large and beautiful. Scientists are interested in Mexican caves because they frequently are different from caves found in temperate zones. The climate inside a cave depends partly on the elevation and latitude of the cave's location. Subterranean climatic conditions also can vary greatly from one part of a cave to another. This is especially true of tropical and subtropical caves.

Environmental Factors and Adaptations

A cave can be as warm as 90° Fahrenheit (33° Celsius) or as cool as 60°F (15°C). Humidity (the amount of water in the air) inside caves, can also vary dramatically. Some Mexican caves are almost dry, while others have a humidity rating above 90 percent. Sometimes, the humidity is due primarily to streams flowing inside the cave. Caves with many bats may have higher humidity because their droppings contribute water to the air. The "subterranean ecosystem," which means plant and animal communities together with their physical environment, is a product of several factors. These include the location of the cave, the kind of rock in which it exists, and the climate and vegetation found above ground.

Plant life within a cave is usually very limited. Green plants cannot grow inside a cave because of the absence of sunlight there. But some other plants, such as mushrooms, do not need sunlight and can survive inside caves.

Because of the shortage of plant life inside a cave, animals are not very numerous under the ground either. Still, Mexican caves have many more animals than caves in temperate zones. Most animals in caves must get their energy from food that is organic material, such as decayed plants and insects. Almost all of this organic material must enter the cave from above ground. Scientists believe that Mexican caves have a relatively high number of animal inhabitants because plenty of food somehow gets into caves.

Cave-dwellers include some kinds of fish, crabs, crayfish, shrimp, scorpions, and bats. But many of these creatures spend part of their time in a cave and part of it above ground. Often, the animals that live in both environments don't appear very different from similar creatures that never enter caves at all.

Opposite page: A spelunker (cave explorer) taking a break in the Pacho Blanco Cave (Chiapas). The caves of Mexico have been repeatedly explored by biological expeditions. These expeditions have helped explain the adaptations of subterranean creatures and have discovered a great deal of information about the animal organisms that lived in Central America in the past. The caves provided a refuge for some animal species whose "relatives" above ground failed to survive when environmental conditions changed.

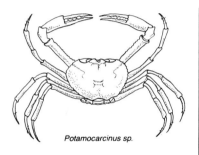

Potamocarcinus sp.

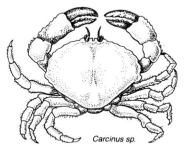

Carcinus sp.

A cave-dwelling crab *(top)* is compared with a noncave-dwelling relative *(bottom)*. The light weight of the body and the elongated legs and claws are particularly evident in the subterranean type. In the dark, the long appendages function like a cane used by a blind person. Similarly, the movements of the cave-dwelling species are slower than those that live in the external environment.

But other animals spend all their time in caves and have adapted so that they can live only in a cave environment. Some of these cave-dwellers have adapted to cave life in surprising ways. Because there is no light in caves to allow animals to see, some of them lack eyes. Others have weak skin or skin with no pigment. Others are extremely sensitive to touch. Many of them would die if they left the narrow range of temperature and humidity found inside a cave.

Sometimes, cave inhabitants can help scientists understand past events. Animals have always used caves as places of refuge during a crisis. If a disaster such as a fire or drought threatened them above ground, they hid in a cave. One example of this happened thousands of years ago when glaciers (huge pieces of moving ice) traveled south along the Sierra Madre mountains. The glaciers moved very slowly and animals migrated in front of them. Some animal species got used to the cool, moist environment near the ice. When the glaciers later melted, the environment became hotter and drier. Some of the animals then began living in caves, where it was also cool and moist.

If the disaster lasted a long time, a species of animal might gradually adapt to living only in caves. For that species, a return to living above ground would be impossible. By examining cave inhabitants today, biologists can learn about the kind of animals that lived long ago. This is especially important because many of these animals have become extinct above ground.

But the environment is not the same everywhere in a cave. Some parts are quite dry while others are wet. Most cave-dwelling animals are adapted for life either on dry ground or in the water. However, a few aquatic species can also exist for a short time out of the water. Because of the high humidity inside a cave, they can spend brief periods searching for food outside of their normal aquatic environment. They must, however, soon return to the water.

Bats, Vampire Bats, and Humans

Bats are among the most interesting cave dwellers. They are mammals, animals that feed their young with milk from the mother's body. They are extremely well adapted for flying at night.

There are at least 154 species of bats in Mexico. These can be divided into eight families and fifty-five groups of related species. They exist in different environments and occupy a variety of ecological niches. Some have become very specialized and can be identified by such characteristics as teeth, body shape, and eating habits. Evening bats, for example, have small bodies, well-developed tails, and eat insects.

Tropical bats are common along the coast, but bats on the plains and plateaus are similar to those found in other places in North America. Their ranges do overlap, however. Many bat species have continued the animal's original habit of eating insects, but others have become eaters of meat or fish. Some eat only pollen and nectar from flowers. One type, the vampire bat, has adapted to eating blood.

Mexico has three species of vampire bats—the common vampire bat, the white-winged vampire bat, and the hairy-legged vampire bat. They all live in the more tropical parts of Mexico, especially in the western Sierra Madre mountains. Vampire bats do not exist outside of Central and

This unique cave-dwelling spider belongs to a group of spiders that is intermediate between true spiders and smaller ones that are specialized for living in cool, humid environments. An odd characteristic of the first group is the presence of a "visor" attached to the front edge of its shell. The animal can raise or lower this structure to cover its mouth and feelers. Furthermore, its epidermis (the outer skin that covers the body) is very thick and appears "sculptured."

South America. Because of its wide distribution, the common vampire bat is the most important and the most feared.

For hundreds of years, human residents of Central America have been aware of the vampire bat's appetite for blood. To get the blood, a bat first makes small cuts in a victim with its sharp teeth. Then it draws out the blood by using its tongue and lips to make a kind of suction tube. Though vampire bats are only about 3 inches (8 cm) long, they can drink as much as 4 teaspoons (20 milliliters) of blood at a time. Usually, a vampire bat's victims will be wild animals or livestock, but they also bite people.

Their most common human victims are farmers. Vampire bats are nocturnal, and they have been known to enter houses that don't have protection against them. Bats can cause serious health problems for humans. Their bites can cause an excessive loss of blood if the victim does not receive medical care immediately. Also, because vampire bats usually attack at night, it often is impossible to get help for a victim quickly. Vampire bats can also transmit rabies.

Cave-dwelling Fish and Aquatic Populations

Fish, shrimp, and crayfish also live in caves. Some species are rather large, and some are blind because of the

Pill bugs and sow bugs are among the most widespread groups of crustaceans. Most of their four thousand species are marine types, but there are also numerous freshwater and land types. The cave-dwelling species make up only a small part of the order. All of the pill bugs and sow bugs have a flat body, a shield-shaped head, and very distinct middle and abdominal body segments. Like all crustaceans, they have two pairs of antennae, one of which is very developed.

Illustrated are areas of distribution of the three species of "blood-lapping" bats *(below)* and the distribution area of a dangerous blood disease that can be carried by these bats *(on the right)*. As the maps show, the disease occurs more often in areas where blood-lapping bats are not found. This leads scientists to believe (contrary to the more common opinions) that bats are not a very important cause, or at least not the main cause, of the spread of the infection.

Following pages: A group of vampire bats is seen in a cave. The blood-lapping bats constitute only a very small minority of bats. Their diet, however, has given a bad reputation to all bats. Actually, most bats are insectivores (insect-eaters). Others are vegetarian and eat only nectar or fruit. Still others are predators of vertebrates, usually small mammals or fish. Finally, only a few are blood-lappers.

lack of light. Some Mexican cave-dwelling fish are extremely similar to fish in other parts of the world. One example is the *Symbranchus infernalis*, a blind fish that is about 12 inches (30 cm) long and one-half inch (1 cm) high. This fish lives in caves in the Yucatán, and a similar species lives in Indonesia. Scientists are puzzled about how two fish species can be so much alike while living so far apart.

Because this kind of research is relatively new, scientists lack precise information about the evolutionary history of these animals. It is probable, however, that they represent the last members of an ancient population that had a very wide distribution. The survivors are true relics of a past that has almost completely disappeared. Perhaps the most famous of Mexican cave-dwelling fish is the blind cave fish. It is just a little more than 2 inches (6 cm) long, has no color, and is practically blind. These little fish are present in a group of caves in a relatively small area, including portions of the states of San Louis Potosi and Tamaulipas. Another unique inhabitant of the underground waters is the *Typhylias pearsi*, a little fish that measures only 3.5 inches (9 cm) in

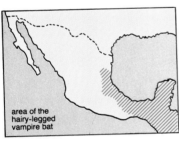
area of the hairy-legged vampire bat

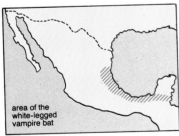
area of the white-legged vampire bat

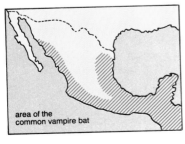
area of the common vampire bat

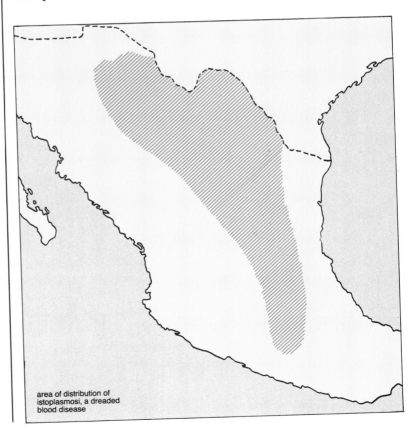
area of distribution of istoplasmosi, a dreaded blood disease

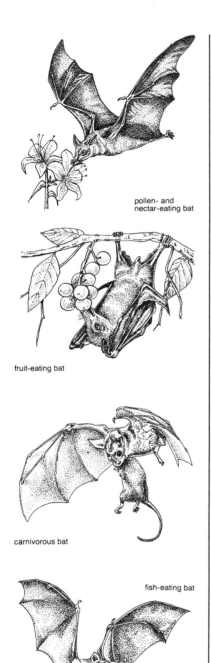

pollen- and
nectar-eating bat

fruit-eating bat

carnivorous bat

fish-eating bat

length. It has well-developed fins on its back and lower rear, and it is completely blind. It is yellowish with rosy shadings, and its scales are small and absent from some areas of its skin.

Cave-dwelling Land Groups

There are many species of cave-dwelling spiders and

scorpions. One of the scorpions present in the states of Tamaulipas and Veracruz is especially well known. This animal is blind and has adapted well to cave life.

Whip scorpions, which resemble scorpions but lack their stingers, are also present in many Central American caves. Many of these species can live either inside or outside a cave.

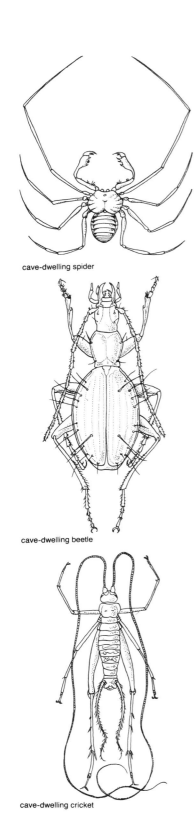

cave-dwelling spider

cave-dwelling beetle

cave-dwelling cricket

Pictured is a blind cave-dwelling fish with no color pigment. Animal species that live underground have little need to maintain certain organs and structures that have lost their function. Once they no longer have a practical function, the organs and structures completely disappear. In the dark environment, these animals move and react using their senses of touch and smell.

Opposite page, right: Shown is the mouth of the Correadero Cave in the forest of the Chiapas. The animals that live in this first cave zone are not completely adapted to subterranean life and are still able to live outside the cave. When outside the cave, however, they prefer to stay in shady, humid environments.

Opposite page, left: Illustrated are three examples of cave-dwelling invertebrates, all of which are able to live exclusively in caves.

Other invertebrates, such as springtails, beetles, and even crickets live in caves. Often, each has adapted in its own way to cave life. The cricket *Paracophus apterus* is frequently found in the caves of the Sierra Madre Oriental. It is easily recognized by its song.

In addition to the true cave-dwelling invertebrates, there are several groups found in Mexican caves that are not cave dwellers in the strictest sense. Many of these animals spend part of their time in caves and part above ground.

THE FOREST

No environment on earth is more fascinating to naturalists than the tropical forest, regardless of whether it lies in Africa, Asia, or America. At the heart of the tropical forest are thousands of giant trees. The canopy formed by the foliage of these enormous trees creates a half-dark, half-light environment. The tree trunks are covered with soft organic matter. Further up the trees hang tangles of epiphytes (nonparasitic plants that grow on other plants). These tangles offer a safe refuge to a myriad of extraordinary life forms.

A Sea of Green

From southern Mexico to Panama, wide areas are covered with large tropical evergreen forests and rain forests. The two most remarkable characteristics of these places are the great variety of species and the remarkable stability of the plant and animal communities. Tropical forests contain immense reserves of biological diversity, a variety of living organisms equaled only on coral reefs. The forest flora and fauna communities have existed here relatively unchanged through many geological eras.

The key to this diversity and stability is the high humidity and plentiful rainfall present in a tropical forest. In the tropical evergreen forest, rain falls for almost half the year. In the rain forest itself, the rainy season lasts even longer. In these moist and warm conditions, trees grow to great height, and a complex vegetative structure emerges on and around the trees.

The enormous trunks of these trees branch out as far as 131 feet (40 m). The canopy layer formed by their upper branches may be as much as 23 feet (7 m) thick. Frequently, thick canopies prevent much of the sunlight from reaching the ground. This upper layer often becomes an environment in itself, and several animal species live almost exclusively in the canopy.

Here and there, a giant tree rises above the rest. This does not happen often, however, because any tree that grows above the canopy becomes exposed to severe weather conditions.

The dense canopy makes it extremely difficult for new plants to begin growing in competition with existing ones. Frequently, the only chance for new trees to get started occurs when an older tree dies and opens up a spot.

Another environment above the ground is sometimes created in the forks of tree branches or in cracks in the tree

Opposite page: The "sea of green" of the Mexican rain forest near Malpaso is shown. The wealth of animal and plant species of these environments has no equal in any other type of habitat on earth. This is due to the enormous productivity resulting from warm temperatures and high humidity and from the wealth of ecological niches available. These niches exist in layers up to 131 feet (40 m) above the ground. However, animals are more difficult to observe in the forest than in open environments. Often naturalists can detect their presence only from their tracks (as in the case of mammals) or from their sounds (as in the case of birds).

Pictured is a typical view of the tropical Caribbean forest. Many of the forests of the West Indies (or the Caribbean Sea) have been destroyed to make room for cultivated crops. The cultivation of crops is necessary to meet the needs of the human population in this region, which has one of the highest growth rates in the world. Very few native forests are protected as parks or reserves. They are often subject to axes, fire, and the guns of poachers.

trunks. Tiny organisms can accumulate in both places, causing the area to appear as though it is covered with a kind of suspended soil. The most common plant species found in these places are bromeliads, orchids, and ferns.

The bromeliads are especially interesting. Because the leaves of these plants are able to hold water at their bases, they attract many species of animals. Amphibians and other animals whose young require an aquatic environment often lay their eggs here. It is not unusual, for example, for frogs to lay their eggs and for tadpoles to emerge in this "minihabitat" many feet above the ground.

The hot, humid, and shady environment that exists on the floor of a tropical forest is well suited to quickly decomposing dead plants and animals. Consequently, these forests are rich with available nutrients, but they do not remain very long in the soil. Almost as soon as a plant or animal decays, the nutrients it contained are recycled into another plant.

Because of the danger and difficulty of moving about on the ground in the forest, some animals have developed new methods of movement. For many, it is especially important to get from one tree to the next. This is made easier by the presence of hanging lianas vines and branches at various distances above the ground. One of the animals best suited to traveling above the ground is the spider monkey. This primate has a long, prehensile tail, which works almost like a fifth limb and can be wrapped securely around branches and vines. By using its tail, the spider monkey can perform acrobatic feats high above the ground.

The connection between land and water environments is quite evident in the tropical forests of Mexico and Central America. Many forests are crossed by large rivers, and numerous animal species are excellent swimmers. Sometimes, a river running through the forest will create the appearance of a tunnel through the thick trees. The top of this tunnel is composed of tree branches 66 to 98 feet (20 to 30 m) off the ground. The most dominant trees in these so-called river tunnels are the *Enerolobium cyclocarpum* and the *Spondia mombin*.

A tropical forest does not always reach a remarkable height and thickness. Where humans intervene or environmental trauma takes place, a secondary forest can be formed. In Panama, for example, secondary forests are largely composed of *Cecropia peltata*, *Miconia argentea*, *Inga punctata*, *Antirrhoea tricantha*, and *Vismia guaianensis*.

Besides rain and evergreen forests, there also are cloud forests at high elevations and conifer forests on high slopes in the more northern mountain ranges. The conifer forests, which are not really tropical, blend into other types of forests, reflecting the great variation of the Central American landscape.

Animals with a southern origin are becoming more and more scarce in the forests of Central America. Every year, there seem to be fewer species in Central America that also exist in South America. This is true for a variety of monkeys,

A magnificent ocelot is surprised by the camera lens of a naturalist in the dense tropical forest. The ocelot, a tree-dwelling animal, spends a lot of time high in the branches, where it catches small mammals and birds, the basis of its diet. It also frequently comes down to the ground, where its keen senses of sight and smell allow it to catch agoutis and pacas. It often stands up on its hind legs and stretches above the grass to hear the sounds produced by potential prey.

birds, butterflies, moths, wasps, and bees. Apparently, many of the animals that originated in the South have evolved into new forms in Central America. This evolution seems to have occurred more recently.

Large and Small Predators

Perhaps the best-known animal in all of Central America is the jaguar. This cat is the American equivalent of the leopard, and it has been featured as a central figure in many adventure stories.

The jaguar stands about 28 inches (70 cm) tall at the shoulder and is about 5 feet (1.5 m) long. Its tail is usually about half the length of its body. The jaguar is the largest feline in all of Central and South America.

This big cat generally lives in areas covered by moist forests and crossed by rivers. It feeds primarily on tapirs, agoutis, porcupines, and other small prey. Occasionally, it catches fish by grabbing them with its claws. At other times, the cat, which is a good climber, hunts birds in trees.

Like many other forest species, the jaguar lives a soli-

kinkajou

raccoon

coati

tary life and is strongly territorial. Adults form pairs during the mating season, but they separate immediately after breeding has taken place. The male plays no part in raising the young.

After a pregnancy of about one hundred days, the female gives birth to two to four kittens. They are extremely vulnerable when born, and the female must nurse them for about six months. Once weaned, however, the young jaguars do not immediately leave their mother. They stay with her for another year and a half as she teaches them how to stalk and kill their prey. Only after this learning period are they capable of becoming independent and capturing their own prey.

Another forest feline is the ocelot, which is a bit smaller than the jaguar. It measures less than 3 feet (1 m) long, and it stands only about 20 inches (50 cm) tall at the shoulders. It is hunted for its beautiful spotted fur.

The ocelot's diet includes small peccaries, paca rodents, agouti rodents, birds, amphibians, and reptiles. It is more arboreal (living in trees) than the jaguar. Because of its extreme shyness, very little is known about the ocelot's reproductive habits.

Two other felines, the margay cat and the wildcat, also inhabit the Central American forest. Both of these animals prefer to live near the forest edge, where one type of habitat blends into another.

There are also various types of smaller predators in the forest, some of which live in trees. The most common of these are the raccoon and its relatives, the coati and kinkajou, plus the cacomistle, and, in the more southern areas, the bush dog. The three types of Mexican raccoons prefer to live in areas with abundant water because they are skilled at catching crabs and fish. The best-known type of raccoon exists throughout all of Central and North America. It is not particularly afraid of people and will often approach human homes and farms in search of food.

This animal has the unique habit of washing its food before eating it. Captive members of this species almost always perform this odd behavior, and wild raccoons also wash their food frequently. Scientists are not certain why the raccoon does this. It may be because the animal needs the extra water it gets this way. Or, it may simply be that the raccoon is washing the mud and sand off its food.

Other species of raccoon, especially those that exist farther south and on the islands off the coast of Mexico, are

53

Shown is a group of white-tailed deer at the edge of the Mexican forest. These elegant hoofed animals are distributed across a wide area that stretches from Canada to Venezuela. They are found in different types of forests, from the colder northern forests to the tropical ones.

less tame. They have the same water habits, however, and their preferred diet consists of crabs and other river invertebrates.

The coati, a member of the raccoon family, and characteristic of Central America, is about 26 inches (65 cm) long and 12 inches (30 cm) tall. Sometimes it dwells in trees. It is largely diurnal, or active during the day, and is omnivorous.

The basic social structure of the coati is the female and her young, which stay with their mother until they are about two years old. Often, several females and their offspring will join together to form a group of about twenty individuals. During most of the year, males are excluded from this group. During the mating season, however, the males fight among themselves for the right to mate with the females, and the winners are allowed to join the female group for a short time.

The kinkajou is another raccoonlike animal that has adapted well to life in the trees of a Central American forest. This little animal is about 18 inches (45 cm) long and weighs up to 6.5 pounds (3 kg). It is amazingly agile because of its prehensile tail and can move easily from tree to tree.

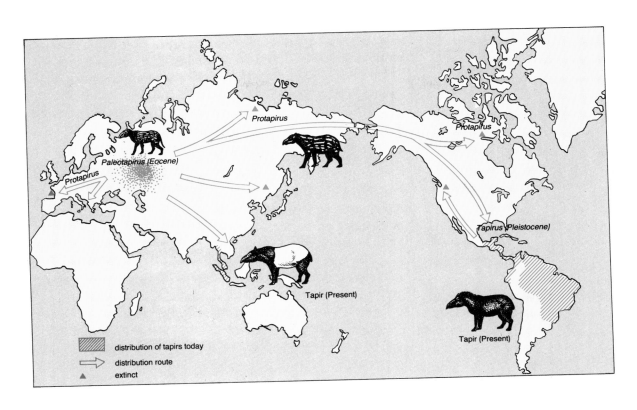

Illustrated are the origin and distribution of tapirs in Southwest Asia and Central and South America. Tapirs first appeared in western Asia nearly fifty million years ago. From there, they spread throughout all of Asia and into North America. After the formation of the Isthmus of Panama, they spread into South America. In more recent times, the tapirs became extinct in all of the temperate zones.

The kinkajou and the binturong of Indochina are the only carnivores in the world that have prehensile tails.

In reality, however, the kinkajou eats little meat, although it does have a preference for insects, which it catches with its long tongue.

The cacomistles also belong to the raccoon family. Both Mexican species of cacomistles have typical raccoon characteristics of being nocturnal and good at tree climbing. One of the two, in fact, virtually lives in trees and even builds its nest there.

Tayras and grisons are also among the inhabitants of the humid forests of southern Mexico. These carnivores resemble weasels and martins.

Another predator, the bush dog, lives as far north in Central America as the Isthmus of Panama. Although this small canine is only 24 inches (60 cm) long and 8 inches (20 cm) tall, it is capable of preying upon rather large pacas. This is possible because bush dogs, like many of their relatives elsewhere in the world, band together for the hunt. Typically, part of the pack lies in ambush, while the remaining members chase the prey toward them.

Other than knowing about the bush dog's teamwork,

scientists have very little information about the animal. Many gregarious (living in groups) species have evolved a complex social organization, but no one knows if bush dogs have done so. Sometimes, this organization includes a system for ranking the authority of each group member, but it's uncertain whether bush dogs have such a hierarchy.

Herbivores at the Bottom of the Sea of Green

Various species of deer, including the small brocket deer, the white-tailed deer, and the mule deer, are common in the tropical regions of the Americas. However, tapirs and peccaries are the most common herbivores, especially in the Mexican forests.

Tapirs are the oldest living perissodactyls, which are animals with an odd number of toes, in the world. Their presence on the American continent is rather recent. Along with their relatives, the horse and rhinoceros, tapirs came here from Asia between 11,000 and 500,000 years ago.

The Mexican species, Baird's tapir, is a stocky animal about 8 feet (2.5 m) long and more than 3 feet (1 m) tall. It can

weigh as much as 770 pounds (350 kg). It has a long snout in which the nose and upper lip are elongated to form a sort of conical trunk. Its coat is reddish brown, and it has a short, dark mane on its neck. Young tapirs have a spotted coat, which enables them to hide more easily.

Although this animal may appear to some people to be rather primitive, it has adapted superbly to the rain forest environment in which it lives. It is a good swimmer and prefers to spend much of its time in or near the water. Tapirs eat a variety of plants, including many aquatic plants which they reach with their long trunks. The animal is not particularly fussy about what part of the plant it eats and will consume leaves, branches, or fruit.

Today, tapirs in Mexico are restricted to the rain forest of Chipas and nearby areas. The animal's survival is in doubt, and the International Union for the Conservation of Nature lists it as an endangered species.

As noted earlier, two species of peccaries, the collared and the white-lipped peccary, live in Mexico. Peccaries, the American equivalent of European wild boars, probably

Shown is a black-handed spider
monkey, which is a Mexican species.
Spider monkeys are typical of the
Central American forests. They occupy
a place similar to that of the baboons,
mandrills, macaques, and langurs of the
Old World.

Opposite page: Other groups of
animals besides monkeys have found it
advantageous to develop tree habits in
the forest. As a consequence, there are
unrelated species having the same
structural characteristics, such as a
prehensile tail. *From top to bottom:* the
spider monkey, tree porcupine (rodent),
and the collared anteater (edentate).

black-handed
spider monkey

tree porcupine

collared
anteater

originated in the northern part of North America. Peccary fossil remains found there date back at least twenty-five million years.

By contrast, peccary fossils in Central and South America are much more recent. This indicates that these animals probably did not reach the southern portion of the Americas until the Isthmus of Panama formed between the two land masses. It's likely, therefore, that the Mexican peccaries are the descendants of the peccaries that migrated south into South America after the isthmus was formed.

Collared peccaries appear to be able to adapt to more types of habitat than the white-lipped variety. Therefore, the collared variety has a wider distribution.

White-lipped peccaries are more aggressive, however. They have upper canine teeth that point downward—just the opposite of European wild boars. White-lipped peccaries are about 3 feet (1 m) long and about 20 inches (50 cm) tall at the shoulder.

They are gregarious, living in herds that sometimes have as many as one hundred members. Herds are able to remain together, it seems, because of an identifying odor secreted by a scent gland on each animal's back. A member of the herd that strays away can find its group again by locating this smell. The scent is also used to mark the herd's territory.

The final group of ground-dwelling herbivores is the rodent. The amazing ability of rodents to adapt to almost any environment has allowed them to spread throughout the Americas. In many cases, several species have evolved from a common ancestor, each one adapting to occupy a separate ecological niche.

Many species probably penetrated the southern subcontinent in successive migrations. Prior to their arrival in some places, marsupials were probably dominant. It's likely that rodents gradually spread from island to island, with new forms evolving in response to particular local conditions.

Pacas, which can reach a weight of 20 pounds (9 kg), are among the largest of Mexican rodents. Their spotted fur allows them to camouflage themselves quite easily in a tangle of vegetation. Pacas are nocturnal and solitary animals that generally prefer watery environments where they can find refuge when danger arises.

Agoutis are rather large rodents, somewhat similar to but more agile than guinea pigs. They are related to several similar species that are predominately South American.

59

The giant ground sloth is an extinct North American sloth that reached up to 15 feet (4.5 m) in length. After the formation of the Isthmus of Panama, this animal spread to Central America, where it quickly became extinct. It had enormous claws that it used to dig in the same way the giant anteater uses its claws today. The giant anteater is considered by scientists to have descended from the giant ground sloth.

giant ground sloth

giant anteater

Agoutis are gregarious, diurnal animals that feed mostly on fruit and live in environments similar to those usually inhabited by pacas.

Mammals of the Tree Layer

The tree-dwelling animals that make the biggest impression on visitors to the forest are monkeys. According to one theory widely held, monkeys arrived in South America between 25 and 36 million years ago. Like other animals, they probably populated the area by moving from one island to the next. This gradual immigration gave rise to sixty or more species in the Amazon region alone, and from there they spread out to even more places.

There are two chief monkey species present in the southern region—spider monkeys and howler monkeys. Spider monkeys are characterized by, and get their name from, their exceptionally long legs and tail, which is prehensile. With these long appendages, spider monkeys make superb climbers and treetop acrobats. One type, the black-handed spider monkey, is about 2 feet (60 cm) long and has a tail of about the same length. It has a light, hairless face that stands out from the grayish yellow of the rest of its body.

Howler monkeys owe their name to the raucous choruses and screeching sounds they make. Though these singing "performances" may sound like so much noise to humans, they have certain social functions. Monkeys use different sounds to create a complex communication network among the group. For example, a mother may need to communicate with her young, or a dominant male may want to give a message to the rest of the group. Also, such communication can be used by one group of monkeys to signal their presence to neighboring groups.

When two potentially hostile groups come into contact with each other, this oral communication may allow them to fight a "bloodless war." Instead of actually fighting, the males conduct a screaming battle, howling louder and louder as if they were trying to make their enemies go deaf.

Such vocal performances are possible because of adaptations in the howler monkey's jawbone and other organs related to its voice. For example, a bone in its throat has evolved into a resonating chamber that produces acoustic waves.

Howler monkeys typically live in groups of about twenty members, which are made up of males and females with young. Each female usually has only one young at a

Glyptodont

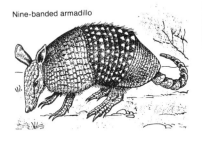

Nine-banded armadillo

time, and the mother looks after that youngster very carefully.

The coendou, or tree porcupine, is another interesting Mexican rodent. It is a tree-dwelling animal that lives mostly in the heights of the forest. This creature is present in Chiapas and the Yucatán, but it is also found as far north as Guerrero and San Luis Potosi. Coendous typically measure about 2 feet (60 cm) in length and have a prehensile tail about 20 inches (50 cm) long. Its body is covered with long needles that make it look like a porcupine. Coendous climb trees with amazing agility in their search for fruit, leaves, and other food.

Many bats also live in the forest. The most common are the plant-eating bats, which feed mostly on fruit, flower nectar, and pollen which they collect with their specially adapted tongues.

Above: The enormous glyptodont, a shelled animal as large as an ox, is compared with its ancestor, the nine-banded armadillo. The glyptodont was captured and perhaps kept in a semidomestic state by the primitive human inhabitants of South America. Like many other species, however, this creature disappeared not long after the joining of North and South America. In fact, some of the most spectacular South American fauna were unable to survive the competition with the new life forms that arrived from the North.

Right: The three-toed sloth lives primarily in the South American forests, but it is also found in the Central American forests as far north as Honduras. Equipped with large, strong claws, it clings to branches with its head down, sleeping most of the day. It moves extremely slowly, which prevents it from being noticed easily.

Pictured is an area of forest in the Yucatán Peninsula. The precipitation in the rain forests is very high at 60 inches (1,500 mm) per year, and it is well distributed throughout the year. This permits vegetative growth that is always luxuriant and supports a surprising variety of species.

Mexican plant-eating bats are strictly tropical animals, and they closely resemble South American long-tongued bats, whose diet also consists mostly of fruit.

Of particular interest to many people are the two species of fish-eating bats found in this region. The fisherman bat is typically found in the tropical forest, and the fishing bat lives mostly around the Gulf of California.

Scientists do not know a lot about the fishing bat. The fisherman bat, however, is known to capture its prey by skimming the surface of running water, both in the forest and on the open sea. Like many other types of bats, the fisherman bat locates its prey with a type of "radar." As it skims the water's surface, it reaches out with its claws and grasps the fish. Then it lifts the prey to its mouth and stores the fish in its cheeks.

Native Forms of an Ancient Population

As mentioned earlier, South America was isolated for a long time, although it did undergo some periods of connection with other continental areas. During the long separations, the original population of marsupial mammals and primitive placental mammals evolved without competition from hardier groups. Placental mammals are those that nourish the fetus while it is inside the body of the pregnant female.

Armadillos, anteaters, and sloths are among the most recent species that provide evidence of the original fauna. They are the survivors of groups that included extremely large animals.

In Central America, the sloth family is represented by the three-toed sloth. Like its relatives, this creature lives in trees, eats only leaves, and rarely ventures to the ground. Sloths are named for the slowness of their movements and the absolute indifference they seem to have for the world around them.

Other tree-dwelling animals include the collared and pygmy anteaters. Unlike their ground-dwelling relative, the giant anteater, these two are quite at home in trees, where they climb with unbelievable skill in search of termites and other insects. The female transports her young by allowing them to grab onto the hair on her back.

South America has numerous species of armadillos, but only the nine-banded armadillo lives in Mexico. This animal originated in South America and has spread as far north as the southern United States. Its northern limit is the

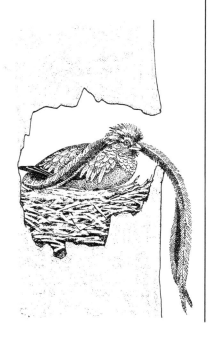

freezing line. This primitive animal is protected by a shell about 16 inches (40 cm) long, although this armor is less rigid than in other armadillo species. With its pointed snout and its relatively large ears, the nine-banded armadillo explores its environment in search of food and is always on the lookout for predators. It is able to dig deep dens, and it feeds primarily on insects, although it will also eat snails, worms, and other small invertebrates.

Opossums are another typical representative of the group of animals that originated in South America. The common South American opossum is perhaps the best known of these animals. This animal lives in a variety of habitats, including areas close to humans. It competes rather well with other more "modern" animals and is, in fact, continually progressing northward.

Another Mexican insect-eating animal is the mouse opossum. This animal is between 3 and 8 inches (9 to 19 cm) long and has a prehensile tail measuring 4 to 12 inches (10 to 30 cm). Mouse opossums generally lead solitary lives, eating fruit and small animals. They are often found on banana plantations, where they can cause great damage, and have inadvertently been transported to other countries in banana shipments.

The Birds

The tropical forest is an ideal habitat for birds, which are among the most fascinating animals in this region. An inexperienced visitor, however, may be disappointed by a quick trip through the Mexican rain forest. At first, the forest seems to be a vast, silent expanse of green, but with patience and perseverance, a visitor will be able to appreciate this world of incredible shapes and colors.

The Mexican forest is the northern limit for many South American species of birds, and it is here that one can observe the differences between northern and southern birds. For example, on the Mexican plateau, most birds are of a northern origin. But along the coasts, at the same latitude, the birds are distinctly South American.

There are about forty-five species of tinamous in all of South America. These primitive birds live on the ground and are related to ostrichlike birds, although their body shape resembles that of a partridge. Because of their peculiar bone structure, they are considered to be the basis of evolution for all birds.

Mexico has four species of tinamous, two of which are

the great tinamou and the little tinamou. These birds move about easily on the forest floor, where they are well camouflaged in their search for seeds and small animals. When they fly, which is rarely, they do so awkwardly and become easy targets for birds of prey.

Tinamou mating behavior is rather unusual. The female initiates the courtship and once mating is over, lays ten to twelve eggs in a nest. However, she then abandons the nest and searches for a new mating partner. The male is left to care for the eggs.

Tinamous are widely hunted for their tender and tasty meat. In the past, there have been attempts to introduce them into game reserves farther north, but these endeavors have not been very successful.

Central America has ten species of curassows, game birds that are closely related to grouse and pheasants. The family to which they belong originated in North America, and some of their characteristics, such as their feet, resem-

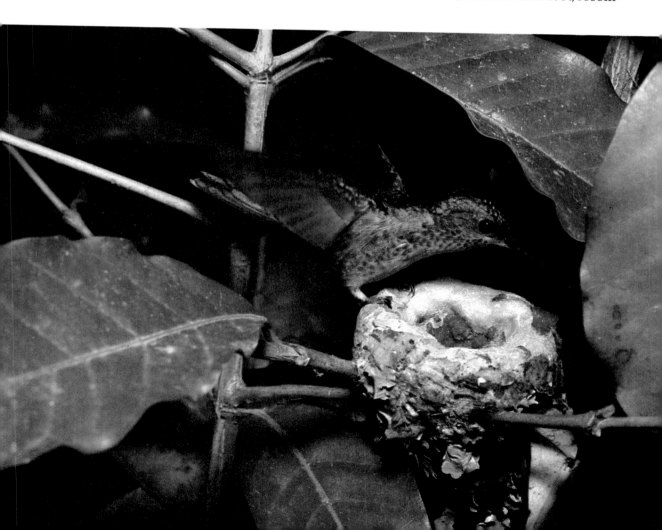

Although the hummingbird differs greatly from the moth (an insect), the two appear extraordinarily similar in the way they hover in the air while sipping nectar from flowers. These two nectar-eaters have evolved in a parallel manner.

ble those of turkeys. They often have a tuft of curled feathers similar to a crest on top of their heads. They make harsh chirping sounds like chickens and resonant sounds similar to those that occur when a person blows over the neck of a bottle. The great curassow and the crested guan are the largest of the Central American curassows.

The small chachalacas live in trees as well as in thickets of shrubs. They are fruit-eaters and build their nests between branches of trees. No more than two or three eggs are laid, and when the male and female are assured of the safety of the eggs, they will abandon the nest to search for seeds, insects, and worms.

Quetzals are famous birds, being symbolic of the forest and of the history of Mexico. They are among the most magnificent and extraordinary of the multicolored trogons, which are birds that have their first and second toes pointed backward. Trogons, peculiar birds with no close relatives, are present in Africa and tropical Asia as well as in Central and South America. Quetzals are about the size of pigeons and have characteristic tufts of feathers on their heads.

A quetzal male has a shiny green head, throat, and breast, a brilliant red belly, and a black-and-white tail. They also have several long green feathers that cover the primary tail feathers. During the mating period, these feathers can reach a length of 3 feet (1 m). Females have more subdued coloration and do not have the exceedingly long feathers.

Quetzals live primarily in rain forests from Mexico to Guatemala, nesting in the cavities of tree trunks that have been excavated and abandoned by woodpeckers. They may also excavate their own nesting cavities in rotting tree trunks, but this does not happen often, because the bird's beak is not particularly strong.

Both male and female quetzals assist in building the nest and hatching the eggs. To incubate the eggs, the male must fold its long tail feathers over its body, making them cover the opening of the nest. In the beginning, the young are fed small animals and insects, but the parents gradually alter the diet until it includes only the fruit and berries that are the normal fare of adult quetzals.

Locally, quetzals are called the "hummingbirds of the mountain" because of their brilliant plumage. In the past, the Aztecs called them "feathered serpents" probably because of their long tails. The Aztecs respected the bird in a religious sense, and they used its magnificent tail feathers to adorn persons of high rank.

Coral snakes are found from the border of Mexico and the United States to Paraguay and Northern Argentina. They have brilliant red, yellow, black, and blue colors. Their fangs, which are similar to those of the cobra, contain a deadly venom. The bright colors of the coral snakes serve to warn predators of their deadliness. However, there are several harmless snakes (called false coral snakes) that have nearly the same colorings. Consequently, they are not often attacked by predators.

Sun-bitterns are also uniquely beautiful birds. The name notwithstanding, this bird is not a true bittern or nocturnal heron, despite a superficial resemblance to bitterns. Actually, it is the only surviving member of another bird family.

One of the most unusual birds of prey of the forest is the harpy eagle, which is probably the most aggressive of all the eagles. It is about 3 feet (90 cm) tall with a black crest and enormous talons. It preys mainly on monkeys, but it also will hunt opossums, deer fawns, medium-sized birds, and occasionally dogs and sheep.

Hummingbirds are also important, and about fifty species inhabit the Mexican forest and sierras. They are among the smallest birds in the world, with some weighing less than one-tenth of an ounce (2.5 g) and measuring just a few inches or centimeters in length. Because they are such small warm-blooded animals, they must maintain a very high rate of metabolism. The heart of a hummingbird may beat as many as one thousand times per minute.

This high rate of metabolism forces them to feed on

Almost all amphibians have at least a trace of toxic substances in their skin. However, arrow-poison frogs have quite a large concentration of poison in their skin. They are found in the forests of Central and South America. The native Indians of the tropical forest used these animals to poison the tips of their arrows, which were used to hunt small mammals and birds. Like many other poisonous animals, arrow-poison frogs have very bright colors, most often yellow, red, or blue.

foods that are high in energy, such as the nectar of flowers. They sip nectar with a specialized long beak while hovering above flowers with an amazing beating of their wings. When hummingbirds are not feeding, they become temporarily inactive in order to reduce their use of energy to a minimum.

Three of the best-known forest hummingbirds are the red-throated hummingbird, green-backed Barrot's hummingbird, and Eloisa's hummingbird. Interestingly, most hummingbirds do not trill or sing, but rather "squeak."

There are many other bird families that live in the tropical forests of southern Mexico. One is the tanager family, colorful birds that inhabit the thickest and darkest parts of the forest. They feed on insects, spiders, millipedes, fruit, and nectar. Other birds worthy of mention are tyrant flycatchers, blue jays, troupials, ovenbirds, antbirds, parrots, and herons.

Reptiles, Amphibians, and Other Animals

Although mammals and birds are undoubtedly the most striking animals in the Mexican tropical forest, there is another world within the forest environment that is rich with fauna. Included here are the reptiles, amphibians, and other animals that constitute the food base for the carnivo-

There are about 1,500 species of bird spiders. The species that are found in the forests of Central and South America have an appearance and size that is truly impressive. Their poison acts on the nervous system of the victim, and it is very strong. Several species of bird spiders can kill a small bird or mouse in a few minutes. Their bite can sometimes be fatal even for humans.

rous species. However, a few of these "overlooked" species also prey on birds and mammals.

Perhaps the most notable of these animals is the boa constrictor, a snake measuring about 16 feet (5 m) in length. This reptile is found from Argentina to Mexico, invariably near water. Boa constrictors can climb trees when necessary, and they do not hesitate to feed on other snakes and rodents.

Numerous other species of snakes have also adapted to living in trees and to preying on the other animals that live above the ground. Some, like coral snakes, are particularly

poisonous. But nature has also provided for the snake's prey. The coral snake is brilliantly colored, which serves to warn prey animals of the potential danger from these deadly serpents.

In turn, the coral snake's bright colors also help others of its kind. Some nonpoisonous snakes have evolved coloration similar to the coral's, and this helps protect them from attack by birds and mammals. Also, there are mildly poisonous serpents that look like coral snakes. When these creatures bite a mammalian or avian predator, the attacker will likely get sick but not die. In this way, predators have learned to avoid most of the snakes that in any way resemble the brilliant coral species.

Another group of forest reptiles includes iguanas and anole lizards, which live chiefly in the trees in tropical forests. Common iguanas have a vegetarian diet and live mainly along streams. When threatened, they jump in the water and swim away. Anole lizards can change colors like chameleons. Basilisk lizards feed primarily on insects and can be identified by the erect crest on the back of the head. Because of their skin color, these animals can hide easily amid the forest vegetation and quickly surprise their prey.

The moist environment of the rain forest is ideal for amphibians. Some even manage to live in trees, where they can take advantage of the water that collects between the basal leaves of the plants called "epiphytic bromeliads" that grow on the trees. These tiny pools of water collect insects, which are the primary food of the tree-dwelling amphibians.

The pools also have enough water to support tadpoles. Many salamanders and tree frogs make their homes in the trees of the tropical forest. Perhaps the most common of these are the red-eyed green tree frog called *Agalychnis callidryas* and another frog with a pointed head called *Diaglena reticulata*.

Many invertebrates also live in the forests. These animals are instrumental in breaking down organic matter such as dead plants and animals into minerals and nutrients that can be used again by plants. For example, virtual armies of ants and termites help decompose dead wood. The high humidity and warm temperatures make this decomposition process go very fast in the tropical forest. The large populations of these invertebrates are held in check by spiders, scorpions, whip scorpions, centipedes, and predatory beetles that are constantly ready to prey on them.

71

Shown are schematic diagrams of the cable system constructed to study the reproductive strategies of the plants in the Finca La Selva Reserve in Costa Rica. With this ingenious system, it was discovered that each "level" of the forest has its own characteristic group of plants and animals, including the pollinating insects. The top two bees in the illustration were found only in the top layers of the forest canopy. The bottom two bees were found only in the lower layers. This layering can result in the genetic isolation of the plants at each stratum, since their flowers are visited only by the pollinating insects of that particular level. These plants thus evolve independently of the similar plants that may live ten or fifteen feet higher or lower.

Bird spiders are perhaps the best known of these animals. They are rather large for spiders, sometimes measuring more than 2 inches (5 cm) in length. With their legs extended, they could cover a medium-sized dinner plate. Besides preying on smaller invertebrates, they also have been known to attack small birds and rodents. Their bite can be deadly even to humans.

The tropical rain forest is also home to harmless and useful insects known as stingless bees. As far back as the days of the Mayas and Aztecs, humans kept hives of these bees for the production of honey. In fact, this species of bees is still kept as a honey producer in many parts of Central America. Hollow tree trunks are often used as hives.

These bees communicate with chemical signals, which is different from the technique used by many other bees.

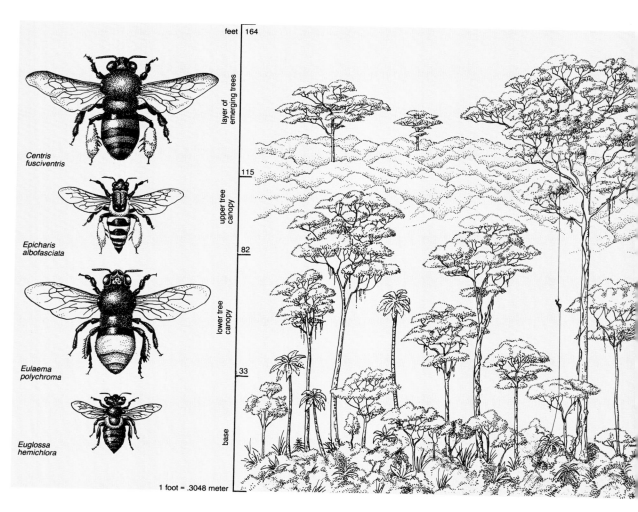

Centris fusciventris

Epicharis albofasciata

Eulaema polychroma

Euglossa hemichlora

feet 164

layer of emerging trees

115

upper tree canopy

82

lower tree canopy

33

base

1 foot = .3048 meter

Bees in Europe and North America, for example, get messages to each other by frenetic movements and through particular flight patterns.

A description of the rain forest would be incomplete without mentioning the fascinating morpho butterflies. The sight of their brilliant metallic colors in the semidarkness of the forest is an unforgettable experience.

And finally, because of the moisture that is usually abundant in the forest, these areas are also home to many creatures that are normally considered aquatic. These include aquatic flatworms and other worms which inhabit the thin film of water covering the leaves and some parts of the ground.

THE AQUATIC WORLD

Mexico is characterized by rough landforms with a rather complicated system of rivers and bodies of water. Actually the country has a plentiful supply of water bodies, particularly in the southern region.

Aquatic and Coastal Environments

Aside from the arid peninsula of Baja California Sur, the Mexican river system can be divided into three large areas—the region whose rivers drain into the Pacific Ocean, the region whose rivers drain into the Gulf of Mexico and the Caribbean Sea, and the arid north-central part of the country.

There are no large major rivers lying totally within Mexico's borders. The greatest portion of the Colorado River, for example, lies within the United States. And the Rio Grande River, which forms the border between Texas and Mexico, is shared by the two countries. There are, however, many long rivers in Mexico, especially near the coast of the Gulf of Mexico.

Various natural and artificial lakes help modify the local climate in some areas. On the central plateau, for example, there are often numerous temporary pools of water which have a large influence on the environmental conditions of the area.

Mexico also has 5,000 miles (8,025 km) of coastline. The Atlantic coast is characterized by wide, sandy beaches, while the Pacific coast tends to be rockier and rougher. The Pacific coast has many lagunas, which are small lakes or ponds, that often extend for some distance and may be filled with mangrove trees. These mangrove swamps give the Pacific landscape its characteristically tropical appearance.

Mexico also has numerous islands, most of which are located near the Lower California peninsula and the Yucatán peninsulas. The total length of coastline of these islands is approximately 740 miles (1,194 km).

Animals of the Continental Waters

Most of the aquatic animals that live in the interior of Mexico have yet to be studied. Even in arid areas, there are numerous forms of aquatic life. Here in these dry places with only a few sources of water, a surprising number of animals live by using the thick vegetation for food and shelter. An interesting example is the area surrounding the small lake San Felipe Xochiltepec in the state of Pueblo. This lake is about 2 miles (3 km) long, about 1.25 miles (2 km)

Opposite page: Pictured is a typical mangrove forest in Central America. Mangrove forests are found in practically all of the tropical regions of the world, often along coasts and estuaries (the place where a river meets the sea).

The brightly-colored cichlid is found in great numbers in Mexican lakes. In the past, it was a traditional dish of the Mexican people. Today, it is a popular aquarium fish.

wide, and less than 10 feet (3 m) deep. The vegetation on the shore and in the nearby area forms such a tight ring around the lake that the body of water appears even smaller. But this vegetation attracts many insects and birds, and they make a good living here in this small circle of abundant life.

The areas of open water on San Felipe are very productive, and in the warm months the visibility in the lake drops to only 20 inches (50 cm) because of the abundant plant and animal life. Fish are very numerous here, especially cichlids, tropical, spiny-finned fish which are also found in many other Mexican lakes. In the past these fish were favorite targets of local fishermen, who caught the fish in fan-shaped nets.

Several salamanders of biological interest also exist in the pools and small rivers of Central America. An example is the mole salamander, whose larvae or newly hatched young are studied in laboratories around the world.

Mole salamander larvae called "axolotls" are of particular interest to scientists because they exhibit the phenomenon of neoteny. Neoteny is the ability to reproduce sexually before becoming an adult.

The axolotl is a mole salamander that lives on land in its adult stage and resembles the North American yellow-and-black salamander. Frequently, the larvae (young stage, *bottom left of the illustration*) of this salamander become sexually mature without changing into the adult form. Thus, they are able to reproduce but continue to live in water and breathe with gills. This phenomenon, called neoteny, seems to be due to the lack of iodine in the lakes where these amphibians live. Iodine is an essential element for the process of metamorphosis (the change from young to adult form).

Mole salamanders resemble European salamanders both in the larval stage when they live almost exclusively in water and in the adult stage when most of their time is spent on land. The adult forms of both species are colored black with yellow spots.

Researchers believe that the phenomenon of neoteny results from the lack of iodine in many lakes and pools throughout Mexico. Because of the lack of this element, the salamander's thyroid gland is not able to produce the hormones necessary to start metamorphosis. Metamorphosis is the changing process that will take the young salamanders from the larval stage to adulthood. In the laboratory, scientists have succeeded in prompting this change in young salamanders by giving them injections of iodine.

Crayfish are unique freshwater animals. Because many Mexican bodies of water have been isolated from other aquatic regions for a long time, many distinct kinds of crayfish have evolved. Four common types are found in cool, clean, running water as well as in reservoirs and in artificial lakes. These water bodies are biologically interesting because they are often inhabited by shellfish such as ostracods, which feed on crayfish.

Shown is a group of Mexican pied stilts in a marsh. The European pied stilt has less black on its head and neck than the Mexican variety. These elegant long-legged birds grace the marshes and lagoons throughout the world.

osprey

caracara

boat-billed heron

Three species of birds commonly found in the area of Mexico and Central America are illustrated. The osprey *(top)*, like the pied stilt, is widely distributed in all the continents of the world; the caracara *(center)* is a falcon that is distributed over Central and South America; the boat-billed heron *(bottom)* is characterized by an unusual beak.

Among the freshwater animals in Mexico, there are certain species that live predominantly in the sea. One example is the nemertine, a small reddish worm about three-fourths of an inch (2 cm) long. This invertebrate is found amid decaying plant matter on lake bottoms or among the shore vegetation. Other examples include several bryozoans, which are small aquatic creatures that reproduce by budding, and several types of sponges. Mammals associated with the aquatic environment are less frequently seen, and their numbers are in serious decline. For example, the Colorado River has become the southern limit where the Canadian otter is found, and the creature is becoming very rare in the north as well.

Another species of river otters, however, has a wider distribution that extends into South America. These fish-eaters are frequently seen confidently and gracefully swimming and diving in estuaries. Estuaries are arms of the sea that extend inland to meet the mouth of a river.

Beavers have already become a rarity in the waters of northern Mexico. But other interesting species, such as the water opossum or "yapok," are more plentiful. This marsupial, which exists from Central America to southern Brazil, is characterized by webbed feet, short, thick, gray spotted hair, and a scaly, reddish tail similar to the tail of an enormous rat. Water opossums reach a length of about 12 inches (30 cm) and are excellent fishers. They live primarily in pools and rivers, where they feed on fish, fish eggs, and shellfish.

Among the numerous species of aquatic birds that inhabit the freshwater wetlands, herons, bitterns, and egrets are the most widespread. Some of the most interesting species are the little green heron, common egret, Louisiana heron, boat-billed heron, and the rare chestnut-bellied heron. The boat-billed heron resembles a black-crowned night heron, except for its considerably larger beak.

A noteworthy member of the stork family, the "jabiru," also makes its home here. This bird is almost 4 feet (1.2 m) long, and its plumage is completely white except for a bare, black head. Its unusual beak enables it to easily capture the fish and amphibians that make up the bulk of its diet.

Several species of North American ducks and geese come to winter in this region, but only a few South American species have their northern limit of distribution here. The large populations of small animals in this kind of environment also attract many birds of prey. Among these are marsh hawks, ospreys, and various caracaras, or falcons.

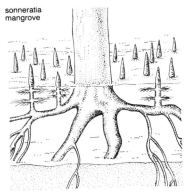
sonneratia
mangrove

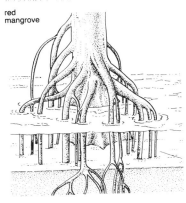
red
mangrove

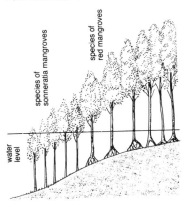
species of sonneratia mangroves

species of red mangroves

water level

There are different species of trees growing in different "layers" of mangrove forests. These layers are determined by the resistance of the tree to the salt content of the water. Thus, there are a series of parallel strips of different vegetation bordering the coastline. The sonneratia mangroves, which have serial roots that grow upward from the mud, grow in the salt water. The red mangroves, whose dense roots grow downward from the trunk, occupy an intermediate strip. In this manner the whole coastal area is occupied.

Caracaras, in fact, are widespread throughout South America. Two species are commonly found in Mexico, red-throated caracaras and crested caracaras. Red-throated caracaras live in small flocks and feed on wasp larvae, which they boldly rob from wasp nests. The birds have no fear of these dangerous wasps because they are able to repel them with their repugnant odor.

The crested caracara is considered the national symbol of Mexico. It is easily identified by the tuft of black feathers on the top of its head. Its unusual diet consists of invertebrate animals and aquatic plants. However, it is not a persistent hunter and it does not feed on carrion, which are dead, decaying animals.

Estuaries and Coastal Lagoons

Estuaries and lagoons, the places where rivers meet the sea, are inhabited by plants and animals that are adapted to withstand changing and unpredictable environmental conditions. For example, in just one day at the bottom of an estuary, the salt content of the water may change more than it does in an entire year in the open sea. In a very short time, the water in an estuary can change from nearly fresh to quite salty.

Furthermore, in the lagoons, the relatively shallow water and the high production of algae cause the water to heat up. This, in turn, can cause increased growth of vegetation in the coastal areas.

The mangrove swamp is one typical habitat found around Central American lagoons. It consists of a wide expanse of trees whose roots emerge from the mud. There are several types of mangrove trees, including black mangroves, red mangroves, white mangroves, and buttonwoods.

The mangrove trees form thick areas of vegetation in which many species of animals take shelter. The animals feed in the muddy areas during low tides, when most of the trunks and roots of the trees are exposed.

Brown pelicans and snakebirds frequently inhabit mangrove swamps. Though they both eat fish, each has its own distinguishing fishing technique. Pelicans dive on their prey using their large bills as nets. Or, they gather in a cooperative group, beating their wings on the surface of the water to frighten fish into shallower areas. Once the fish have been driven into shallow water, they are easily captured by the pelican team.

A snakebird, on the other hand, captures fish by using

Illustrated are several typical animals of the estuaries and lagoons of Central America. *From left to right:* the caiman, the magnificent frigate bird, the hawksbill turtle, the skimmer (shown in its characteristic fishing flight), a male elephant seal, and the American manatee (in the water).

its long, sharp beak as a harpoon. Specialized neck bones help it launch the beak toward the target. After piercing the fish, the snakebird leaves the water, tosses the fish in the air and swallows it. Cormorants, which are also able fishers, are widespread in these areas as well. The double-crested cormorant and the olive-green cormorant are the most commonly found.

Another common inhabitant of the lagoons and especially of the muddy shores periodically exposed is the fiddler crab. The several species of this strange animal are characterized by a difference in shape between males and females. This difference is called sexual dimorphism. In the male, one of the two pincerlike claws is much larger than the other. In females, however, both claws are equal in size.

Typically, the male's large claw is brighter or lighter in color than the generally muddy color of the rest of its body. When the male crab rhythmically moves its large claw in

Following pages: A large ghost crab has just captured a newborn green turtle. Many sea turtles are killed by predators in the first months of life. These predators include birds, mammals, fish, and even large invertebrates. When one adds to this the extensive hunting of sea turtles and their eggs by humans, it is easy to understand why several species are now in danger of extinction. In several biological stations, the newborn sea turtles are gathered and raised until they reach a large size. This lessens the chance that they will be killed by predators.

the sunlight, it creates a sparkling effect. The male does this to mark its territory and to entice the female into following him into the hiding place he has dug in the mud.

In 1961, several naturalists discovered manatees in a wild, untouched area of the Yucatán Peninsula. This unusual large aquatic mammal lives in fresh water near the coast. Adults can weigh up to 440 pounds (200 kg) and exceed 10 feet (3 m) in length. The manatee is a herbivore and devours enormous amounts of water hyacinths.

The rare Morelet's crocodile is another inhabitant of the coastal lagoons. It can reach a length of 8 feet (2.5 m), and can also live in fresh water.

On the Seashore

The different environments of the Mexican coasts are of great interest biologically. They vary from the rocky coasts near Acapulco to the sandy beaches of the Gulf of

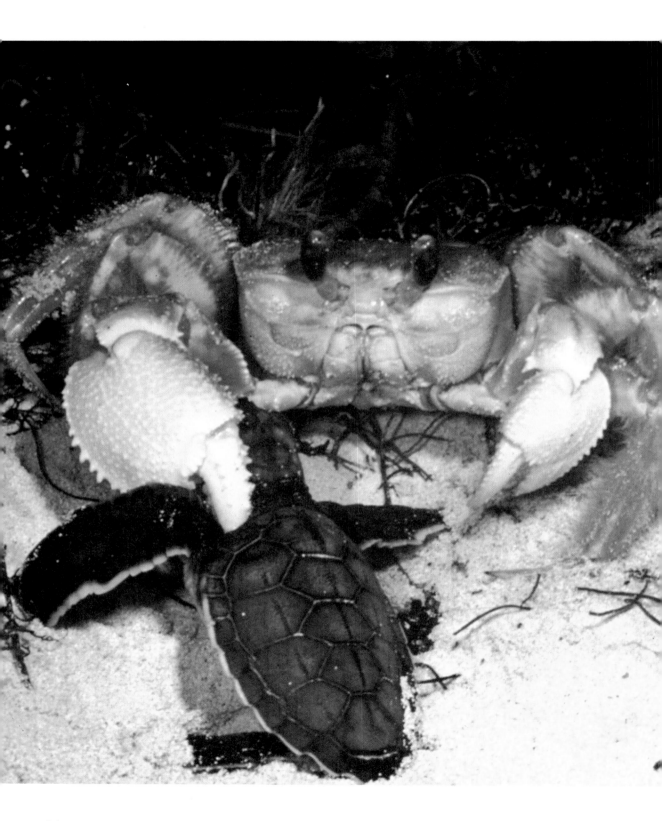

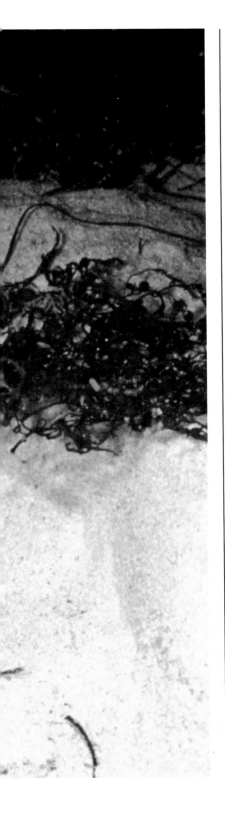

Mexico. The coasts, which are home to many marine organisms with a variety of forms and habits, can be divided biogeographically into different zones.

Generally, the coasts of the Gulf of Mexico and the Yucatán constitute the Caribbean zone. The Pacific coasts are included in the Panamanian zone. And the California zone is composed of the Lower California peninsula.

These distinctions are helpful in reaching a better understanding of the different flora and fauna of these areas and of the way in which species combine in a given habitat. When the Isthmus of Panama was formed in the Pliocene epoch two to thirteen million years ago, the continuity of relationships between the western and eastern coasts of the two American continental land masses was interrupted.

Near the sandy coasts, there typically are a series of strips running parallel to the beach. Each strip has its own characteristic life forms. As the plants and animals gradually became less dependent on the sea, they became more exposed to the atmosphere.

The areas bordering the sea are where life on land began in this part of the world. Gradually, through evolution, some animals became less dependent on the sea environment and more capable of living in a terrestrial environment. Today, several primitive species in this area still provide evidence of that process. For example, ghost crabs are common along the beaches. Though essentially aquatic, these creatures long ago adapted to life out of the water.

Ghost crabs, which are found in tropical areas throughout the world, dig holes in the sand into which they flee whenever they are threatened. As soon as danger has passed, however, the crabs come out of the holes and resume their search for food which consists of dead animals that have washed ashore.

The *Gecarcinus quadratus* is another species of crab that is not tied to the water environment. This crab, in fact, even ventures into the forest. Like other land crabs, this animal has a cavity around its lungs which is able to use atmospheric oxygen without drying out.

Many species of birds are also found along the beaches. Some live permanently in this area, while others are attracted periodically by the abundance of available food. Included in this group are gulls and shorebirds such as dowitchers, dunlins, western sandpipers, and semipalmated plovers.

Another is the skimmer bird, which resembles a large tern. This bird is especially interesting because of its fishing techniques. As its name implies, the skimmer bird catches its prey by flying just above the surface of the water with its jaw open. In fact, the bird's lower jaw is often under the water. As soon as a fish is scooped in, the skimmer bird closes its jaw and swallows the prey. This unusual operation is made somewhat easier by the bird's long lower jaw and relatively short upper jaw.

In contrast to the identifiable strips of the sandy beaches, rocky coasts have a mixed variety of animal inhabitants. Two examples of marine life in these areas are a type of Mexican spiny lobster and the peculiarly shaped box crab. Both of these animals live in the cracks of rocky reefs along the coasts. The box crab is a predator of hermit crabs. With its strong claws, the box crab can easily break open the hermit crab's shell.

There are also many species of marine snails and clams that have an interesting geographical distribution. These include the large abalone, limpets, chitons, and numerous types of bivalves. Bivalves are animals with a shell consisting of two hinged parts. Square-backed crabs,

Three female elephant seals sun on a beach. There are two species of elephant seals found in the Pacific Ocean. One is distributed in the Northern Hemisphere, while the other lives in the Southern Hemisphere. The northern species was on the verge of extinction, but protective measures are resulting in a comeback. In both species, the males grow very large and fight among themselves for the harem of females. This group of females numbers from ten to over one hundred.

in their beautiful reddish colors, are also commonly found on the emerged parts of the rocky reefs.

Tiny springtail insects, which are so small that they can be seen only with a magnifying glass, live along the rocky coasts just inland from where the waves reach. These small creatures originally lived entirely on the land, but they have adapted quite well to a life at the edge of the sea. They are closely related to species that are found in Jamaica and on the European coasts.

The rocky coasts are also home to large numbers of many species of birds. Some birds use these areas as places of refuge during migratory flights, while others nest in the secure areas provided by the rocky cliffs. Birds frequenting these areas include pelicans, grebes, various gulls, boobies, oystercatchers, and frigate birds. Many of them spend at least part of their time fishing on the open sea.

Seals and sea lions also take refuge on the Mexican coast, especially during reproductive periods. Whales and dolphins also enter the bays of Lower California to reproduce.

THE WEST INDIES

The West Indies is composed of the large and small islands of the Caribbean sea. They are actually the peaks of a large chain of submerged mountains which lie outside the Gulf of Mexico. The nature of the islands' interior became known only after the second voyage of Columbus. The total surface area of this archipelago or group of islands is about 100,000 sq. miles (259,000 sq. km). The West Indies is divided into three groups of islands. They are the Greater Antilles, which are halfway between Florida and South America; the Bahamas, which are closer to Florida; and the Lesser Antilles, which are closer to South America.

Islands of Volcanoes and Earthquakes

Although the Greater Antilles do not show traces of recent volcanic activity, the Lesser Antilles are actually a chain of active volcanoes. In fact, the volcanic activity of the Lesser Antilles is matched at very few other places in the world. Only the Aleutian Islands near the coast of Alaska, Japan, and the Sonda Islands in Southeast Asia may possibly have more volcanic activity. For example, Mount Pelée, one of the most famous and active volcanoes in the world, is located in Martinique across from the village of St. Pierre. Its eruptions are remembered as some of the most catastrophic natural events of ancient and modern history.

This volcano's eruptions were burying entire cities long before Columbus ever sailed to this part of the world. After a period of activity, the volcano lay dormant for centuries until May 8, 1902, when it suddenly became active again.

Volcanoes have also caused damage on the nearby island of Guadeloupe, even though the disasters there never reached the proportions of the one at St. Pierre. For example, the volcano Soufrière erupted in 1943 and, along with an earthquake, killed at least two thousand people in about two minutes. Since then, the volcanic activity has largely restricted itself to smoke holes and hot springs. No one knows, however, when the next volcano may erupt on these beautiful islands.

The Climate

The West Indies is located between 10 degrees and 28 degrees north latitude. The average sea level temperature during summer is about 80°F (27°C), and even in the coldest months it rarely drops below 70°F (21°C).

Rainfall, which is influenced significantly by topogra-

Opposite page: Pictured is a beach of the Virgin Islands in the Caribbean. The so-called West Indies includes all of the small and large islands of this area and are characterized by a particularly mild climate. The name of these islands resulted from the discovery of one of them, San Salvador, by Christopher Columbus in 1492.

Cyclones are very violent atmospheric depressions that are characteristic of these islands. They are caused by winds with different speeds and temperatures that blow in opposing directions. The warm air masses form a front against the cold air masses *(top)* while progressively rising. This causes a strong decrease in pressure, which increases the wind speed and accelerates the circulation of the cyclone in a counterclockwise direction *(center)*. The cold air that fills the depression caused by the rising warm front provokes the speedy breakup of the cyclone *(bottom)*.

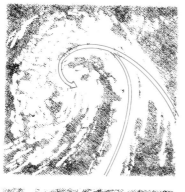

phy (variations in the earth's surface) and by geographic location, shows much more variety than the temperature. For example, in the mountainous areas of the Dominican Republic and Martinique, the annual rainfall ranges from 83 to 87 inches (2,100 to 2,200 mm). In contrast, Barbados, which is not mountainous, has a maximum annual rainfall of about 55 inches (1,400 mm).

Seasons are fairly distinct in the West Indies, however. Winter is dry and cool. Spring and summer are also dry, but the temperature rises steadily through this period. Fall is humid, and during this season violent hurricanes and cyclones can hit the Antilles. These storms are caused by circular winds that blow over areas of low atmospheric pressure. Wind speed inside these storm cells can exceed 125 miles (200 km) per hour.

The Origin of the Island Plants and Animals

The origin of the biological population of the islands was strongly influenced by the formation of their environment. Islands such as the Bahamas are no longer connected to a continent as a result of the rising of the sea level. The plants and animals of these islands are similar to those of the lands with which they were originally connected.

This is especially true if the islands have been isolated from the mainland for a relatively short period of time. A similar result occurs when a continental mass fragments, or breaks up, into smaller islands during the shifting of the earth's crust. Scientists believe that this is the way the entire group of the Antilles islands was formed.

Islands also may form as a result of volcanic activity. These islands, of course, do not have any native flora or fauna. Instead, plants and animals gradually spread to these islands from other nearby places. The best example of this type of island is the famous volcano Krakatoa in Indonesia. There does not seem to be an island of this type in the Antilles.

The number of species present on an island seems to be closely related to the island's size. Among a group of similar islands, those having the largest surface areas also will have the most plant and animal species. Other factors, however, can influence this condition. These include the island's topography, the amount of available fresh water, and the distance of the island from continental land masses. This latter factor has a strong bearing on the possible migration of species.

The number of species that an island eventually ends up with is roughly the number of immigrations it has minus the number of extinctions that occur. Sometimes, this balance can shift dramatically with the introduction of just one or two new species. For example, certain animals might establish a population on an island and thrive there because they have no natural predators. Consequently, this species might fail to develop defensive mechanisms that could assure its survival. If significant predators such as humans and the cats, dogs, and rats associated with them arrive later, the defenseless species could suffer. In fact,

The extraordinary plants of the cactus family originated on the American continent, particularly in the Central American area. Different varieties of these plants are used as houseplants around the world.

The Cuban macaw was a beautiful reddish orange parrot with blue wings, measuring about 20 inches (50 cm) tall. This bird was widely hunted by native people even before settlers began capturing young birds to be sold as pets. This practice and the destruction of its habitat led to the extinction of this magnificent bird in the second half of the nineteenth century. All that remains are a few stuffed birds in museums of natural history.

many island species have become extinct for this very reason.

The Vegetation of the Antilles

Each island of the West Indies has its own characteristic plants, even though the entire archipelago, if taken as a whole, has several common types of vegetation.

The most common plants on all the islands are the red and black mangrove trees. These trees often cover large coastal areas, giving rise to the humid environment usually associated with the tropics. Spiny shrubs, cacti, agaves, and spurges grow in areas where the precipitation is less abundant. The "tree of death" is a well-known spurge that grows to a height of 16 to 20 feet (5 to 6 m). Like all the plants of the spurge family, this one secretes a caustic sap. The sap is poisonous enough to be used on the tips of arrows for hunting, and that is how the name "tree of death" originated.

In the zones with moderate rainfall, there are thickets of shrubs that resemble those commonly found in the Mediterranean regions. In the more humid zones, especially between elevations of 980 and 3,280 feet (300 and 1,000 m), there are rain forests. Here, the trees reach heights of 100 to 130 feet (30 to 40 m) and are often covered with mosses and encircled by liana vines. As has been previously mentioned, the size and the humidity of an island are important factors in determining the number of species present. For example, while there are 8,000 species of plants on the island of Cuba alone, there are only 5,000 species in all of the Lesser Antilles islands. There are also large differences between one island and another. For example, there are 2,000 species of plants in Guadeloupe, 1,800 in Martinique, but only 500 on the small island of St. Martin.

The number of native species is not great. Of the 1,700 species of plants that have been catalogued in the French West Indies, only 165 are native. This relatively low number probably resulted from the geographic position of the Lesser Antilles, which acted as a bridge between the islands and the South American continent. Also, volcanic catastrophes could easily have caused the extinction of native species that had a limited distribution.

The Animals of Cuba

Cuba is the largest island of the Antilles, and it also has the largest variety of plant and animal life. There are an estimated 300 species of birds, 80 species of reptiles, 30

The solenodons are unique insect-eating mammals that resemble enormous shrews in appearance and habits. Their numbers have been greatly reduced as a result of habitat destruction and the introduction of predators to the islands that they inhabit (Cuba and Haiti). The new predators, such as cats and mongooses, were brought by the Europeans. In spite of this, the solenodons have managed to survive to the present day, and it is hoped that they can continue to live in the future.

species of amphibians, 24 species of bats, 4,000 species of mollusks (such as clams, oysters, snails, squid), and 17,000 species of insects.

Several coastal lagoons, such as the Cenega di Zapata, are inhabited by many Cuban crocodiles, one of the few native species. And in the rivers lives the manatee, a large aquatic mammal that may have provided the foundation for the mythical existence of mermaids.

Other spectacular species are now extinct. One is the beautiful Cuban macaw, a magnificent red-and-yellow parrot that was last seen in 1885. Another is the West Indian shrew, which lived in Puerto Rico, Haiti, and the Isle of Pines near Cuba. This small rodent probably became extinct soon after the arrival of the Spaniards several centuries ago.

The Cuban solenodon is another species that has been close to the same fate. The only close relative of this ratlike rodent is found in Haiti. The only animal that the Cuban solenodon resembles is the now-extinct West Indian shrew, whose fossil remains have been studied by zoologists.

The Cuban and Haitian solenodons are insectivorous

and are about 12 inches (30 cm) long with a 10-inch (25 cm) tail. They use their pointed snouts to search for prey. They kill their victims by biting them with their strong teeth and by injecting poison produced by glands under their jaws. When the animals mate, the female builds a simple nest in which one or two young are born.

The Cuban solenodon was discovered in 1535, but it was not described in scientific terms until the first half of the nineteenth century. For a time, it was thought to be extinct, primarily because of human alteration of its habitat. Also, when humans introduced exotic predators, such as the mongoose, to the islands to kill snakes and rats, many solenodons were killed as well. At the beginning of this century, however, some live specimens were rediscovered.

Cuba has many other interesting animals, such as the world's tiniest frog, the *Sminthillus limbatus*, which is less than half an inch (1 cm) long. The female of this strange frog produces a single egg in which the tadpole undergoes complete metamorphosis into an adult form before emerging.

Some mollusk species are only found in Cuba or are

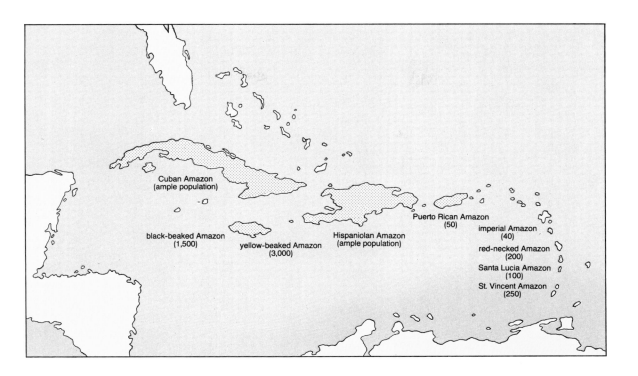

The map shows the distribution and population of several parrots of the Caribbean islands. Their current decline can be traced to deforestation, poaching, stealing from the nests, illegal selling, predation, competition with introduced species, and the violent hurricanes which occasionally strike this area.

limited to the area of the Antilles. Central and South American forms seem to predominate, and many of these are not found in nearby Florida. This could indicate that the introduction of the majority of the mollusk population occurred across the Yucatán Peninsula or perhaps across the Lesser Antilles.

Several freshwater and land shrimp are interesting examples of the biogeographical connections of the animal populations of Cuba and the Antilles in general. The small freshwater shrimp *Atya lanipes* is also found in Puerto Rico. Another species, *Jonga serrei,* is rather widespread in the Antilles and in Costa Rica. The other six members of the family are either native to Cuba, or they have a distribution that is exclusive to the Antilles or to Central America.

Other Typical Animals of the Antilles

Birds are usually the most visible animals in any region of the world. In the area of the Antilles, there are several bird species that are quite typical, such as hummingbirds and todies. The latter are graceful birds which measure about four inches (10 cm) long and are distantly related to kingfishers.

Other very characteristic birds of the region include

Shown is a characteristic view of the beautifully colored fish populating the sea bottom near the island of Trinidad. Because of its geological characteristics and its particularly tropical climate, Trinidad is considered to have the most South American colored fish of the West Indies.

parrots. Many parrot species are present, some of which are native. The most interesting and symbolic of these are the beautiful Amazon parrots. They are rather stout birds with short tails and plumage that is mostly green. The forehead plumage is generally bright yellow, blue, or red.

The reptiles of the Antilles have been more fortunate than the birds. There are many lizards of the iguana family that are common and widespread. Among the most notable lizards are the large knight anoles of Cuba, the anoles or false chameleons, and the ameivas. Anoles are able to change color like chameleons.

Trinidad: A Bridge to America

This island of 1,863 sq. miles (4,825 sq. km) is located directly across from Venezuela. Trinidad is separated from Venezuela only by the two narrow tongues of the Gulf of

Paria. Trinidad has rich deposits of petroleum which can spring forth spontaneously. The characteristic lake of pitch near La Brea always has bubbling liquid at its center, which is used to produce asphalt. The subsoil is also rich with petroleum, which is exported in large quantities.

There are many animal species here that are typically South American, such as the arboreal anteater and the manakin birds. The males of the manakins have a showy plumage of red, yellow, or blue feathers.

A short distance northeast of Trinidad lies the island of Tobago. Its 70 sq. miles (182 sq. km) are still covered by dense forests. This island is like a small tropical paradise. Birds of paradise make their home in Tobago. They were introduced many years ago from New Guinea.

GUIDE TO AREAS OF NATURAL INTEREST

The establishment of national parks and protected zones in Central America has perhaps been a little slower compared to other areas of the world. Nevertheless, today a lot is being done to rapidly make up for this delay. In the majority of cases, however, the internal organization of the protected areas is not yet set up for facilitating tourist visits or longer stays for the purpose of study.

In many cases, areas were put under protection after substantial amounts of damage had already been done to the environment. In the Antilles, for example, the arrival of European settlers and their animals (dogs, cats, rats, pigs, and so forth) caused a great deal of damage to several native species. Studies have pointed out that the number of extinct species or those in danger of extinction on the islands is directly related to the amount of deforestation. For example, in Hispaniola (the second largest island of the Greater Antilles, divided into Haiti and the Dominican Republic), where vast forests still exist, bird communities are fairly intact. But in the Lesser Antilles, where the covering vegetation has changed greatly, there have been from two to four species extinctions on each island.

A visit to the areas of natural interest should be carefully planned, keeping in mind that a journey to these places carries the risk of contracting infectious tropical diseases. Several vaccinations are necessary before departing. There is also a certain amount of risk involved with entering areas of social unrest. In some nations of Central America, armed conflicts are currently taking place.

Unless the visitor can rely on extensive travel experience or on local assistance, it is best to make use of a specialized travel agency. A good example is the National Audubon Society of New York (950 Third Avenue, N.Y., 10022), which each year organizes nature-oriented tours to Mexico and other nations of Central America.

A trip to Cuba should be organized by professionals. Cuba is not represented in this guide to areas of natural interest, since precise information is not available on its two national parks.

In the Antilles and generally in all the islands of the Gulf of Mexico, the climate is rather pleasant for most of the year. But in many areas in the summer, the temperature becomes unbearably hot. In the sierras the nights are always cool, and in the winter they can be quite cold.

Always take the maximum precautions while traveling in these areas.

Opposite page: Shown are two of the pointed peaks of the island of Santa Lucia. These peaks are covered by vegetation. The foreground shows a close view of this tropical vegetation, which includes wild and introduced plant species. It is easy to see why these Caribbean islands came to be regarded as an exotic paradise.

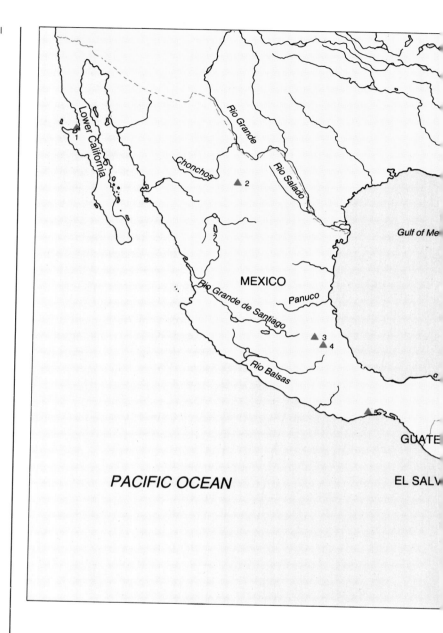

MEXICO

Guerrero Negro
Ojo de Liebre (1)

Mapimi (2)

This nature reserve is located on the coasts of the Peninsula of Lower California, and it has an area of 1,544 sq. miles (4,000 sq. km). It is made up of coastal lagoons and of a strip of land. This is one of the sites to which the gray whales come to reproduce in large groups. The saltwater zone hosts many species of aquatic birds.

This reserve of 85 sq. miles (220 sq. km) is located

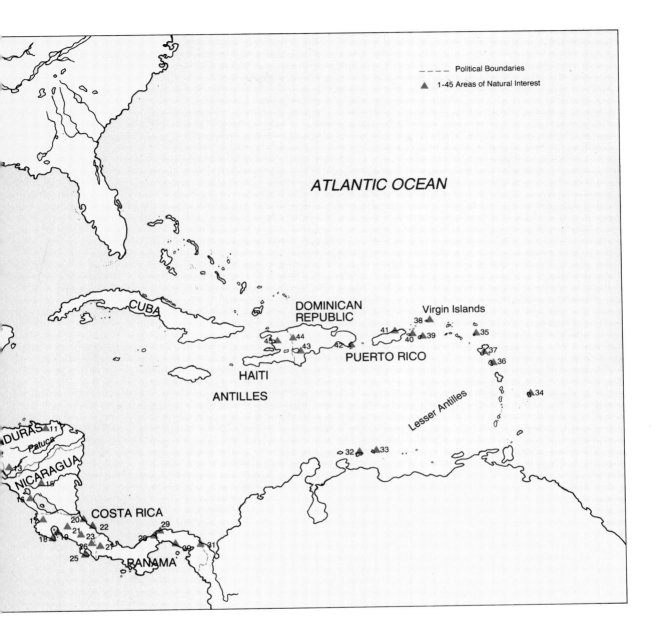

between the states of Durango, Chihuahua, and Coahila at an altitude of about 3,960 feet (1,200 m). It is in a basin surrounded by small mountains, northeast of the city of Ceballos. The vegetation is of an arid type, with several native plant species. With the disappearance of the pronghorn antelope, the reserve lost one of its most interesting animals.

However, there are still pumas, coyotes, bobcats, mule

deer, and gopher tortoises, which are in danger of extinction. The reserve has been the subject of ongoing research since it represents an excellent example of an arid type of biotope.

Lagunas de Zempoala (3)

This national park of 18 sq. miles (47 sq. km) is located between the states of Mexico and Morelos at a rather high elevation. The highest point is 12,800 feet (3,900 m). The park contains seven lakes which were formed in the lava rock of Huilote Volcano. The average annual temperature is 54°F (12°C). At an elevation of about 13,120 feet (4,000 m), the average annual temperature is 41°F (5°C). The annual precipitation reaches 59 inches (1,500 mm).

The luxuriant forest vegetation is composed of oaks in the lower elevations and pines, spruces, and firs higher up. Animals inhabiting the park include the volcano rabbit, a species of rattlesnake, and the ajolote, an amphibian of the mole salamander family.

Iztaccihuatl-Popocatepetl (4)

This national park of 100 sq. miles (257 sq. km) is located in the Sierra Nevada between the states of Mexico, Puebla, and Morelos, at an altitude of about 13,120 feet (4,000 m). It includes the two volcanos from which the park derives its name. Popocatepetl Volcano reaches an elevation of 17,888 feet (5,452 m). The vegetation is composed primarily of conifer forests and alpine meadows. Above 15,420 feet (4,700 m), the mountain slopes are covered with snow all year long. The most interesting animal in the park is the volcano rabbit, a species seriously threatened with extinction.

Montes Azules (5)

This nature reserve is located in the state of Chiapas, in Southeast Mexico. Its large area, 1,278 sq. miles (3,312 sq. km) is dotted with many small lakes which formed in the limestone soil. These lakes are surrounded by low hills covered by luxuriant forest vegetation. Some of the mammals that live here include jaguars, margay cats, ocelots, collared peccaries, Baird's tapirs, black-handed spider monkeys, and mantled howler monkeys. Some of the birds found in the reserve are the harpy eagle, the scarlet macaw, and a species of curassow. Morelet's crocodile thrives in the waters of the reserve.

GUATEMALA

Pecaya Volcano (6)

This protected area of nearly 8 square miles (20 sq. km)

is classified as a national monument. It is situated at an elevation between 4,265 and 8,530 feet (1,300 and 2,600 m), and it can be divided into several strips according to the different altitudes. Up to 4,920 feet (1,500 m) of elevation the dominant plants are soursop trees, silk-cotton trees, and Lusitania cypress. Between 4,920 and 6,890 feet (1,500 and 2,100 m), the predominant trees are Honduran ash, *Cedrela pacayana*, and *Eurya theoides*. Above 6,890 feet (2,100 m), there are isolated areas of a native species of oak, alder trees, and two species of pine. There is quite a variety of animals, including mammals such as coyotes, gray fox, kinkajous, opossums, raccoons, long-nosed monkeys, white-tailed deer, wildcats, and margay cats. An interesting dove species lives in this park, as well as many species of birds of prey whose numbers have not yet been determined.

Rio Dulce (7)

This national park, whose boundaries have not yet been established, is located in the Sierra de Mico. It covers an area of 93 sq. miles (241 sq. km), and it includes Lake Izabal and the mouth of Rio Dulce, the park's namesake. Some of the plants found here are mahogany trees, *Cedrela mexicana*, *Calophyllum brasiliense*, Caribbean pine, and a variety of palm trees. Many interesting animals make their home in Rio Dulce, including manatees, spider monkeys, jaguars, ocelots, raccoons, Baird's tapirs, and white-tailed deer. At least 303 species of birds have been counted in the park. Reptiles include Morelet's crocodile, the American crocodile, and several species of turtles and snakes. There are also at least twenty-eight different families of fish.

Biotope for the Conservation of the Quetzal (8)

This relatively small area of 3.5 sq. miles (9 sq. km) is located in the department of Baja Verapaz in the Sierra de las Minas, at an elevation between 4,920 and 7,710 feet (1,500 and 2,350 m). It was established as a reserve by the University of San Carlos specifically for the protection of the quetzal. The reserve includes two mountains—Cerro Geomaya, 7,704 feet (2,348 m) and Cerro La Cumbre, 6,598 feet (2,011 m). The Colorado River runs through the park, creating a beautiful waterfall. There is an extensive mountain type of rain forest, or cloud forest, with trees over 100 feet (30m) tall. Besides the quetzal, there are at least sixty other species of birds. Twenty-four species of mammals here include howler monkeys, squirrels, Mexican porcupines, reptiles and amphibians, and a large variety of invertebrate animals, which are presently being studied.

Shown is a picturesque view of Lake Atitlan in Guatemala. The volcano in the background has the same name. This lake and the mountains that surround it are one of the Central American zones in which the original plants and animals have been most successfully preserved.

Tikal (9)

This large national park of 222 sq. miles (576 sq. km) is located in the northern part of the country in an area where numerous archaeological remains of the Mayas are found. Here one can find fifty-four species of mammals, such as spider monkeys, giant anteaters, ocelots, margay cats, jaguars, tapirs, and pumas. There are 303 species of birds and many reptiles, including Morelet's crocodile, coral snakes, several species of rattlesnakes, and at least thirty other species of snakes. Interesting large invertebrates and amphibians also inhabit the park.

BELIZE

Guanacaste Park (10)

This small bird sanctuary of 51 acres (0.21 sq. km) is located in Central Belize where the Belize River meets its tributary, Roaring Creek. This sanctuary is of interest due to the numerous species of birds that live here. In the dense forest vegetation, one can also find fascinating iguanas and butterflies. About thirty species of epiphytic plants (orchids, bromeliads, etc.) grow on the trunks of the forest trees. Among the most notable birds here are tanagers, hummingbirds, woodpeckers, and jays.

HONDURAS

Olancho (11)

This large forest complex of 3,860 sq. miles (10,000 sq. km) extends from sea level to an elevation of 3,963 feet (1,200 m). Humid tropical forests grow on the mountain slopes up to an elevation of 4,265 feet (1,300 m) and along the Patuca River. Many animal species still inhabit this area, even though their presence is threatened by the progressive reduction of forest habitat. There are five species of cats (jaguars, ocelots, margays, pumas, and wildcats), Baird's tapirs, and white-tailed deer. Some of the notable birds are beautiful scarlet macaws and military macaws.

Tualabe (12)

The caverns of Tualabe, a national monument, are quite interesting for those who enjoy exploring caves. One can walk for almost 2 miles (3 km) in this underground system of caverns, where some sections are 100 feet (30 m) tall. The entrances are located 2,297 feet (700 m) above sea level in a humid subtropical forest environment of Caribbean pines and Cecropia trees. Some scattered areas are under cultivation. The principal cave entrance leads to a system of underground passages, of which an area of 3,050 feet (930 m) has been explored. The caverns were formed in sedimentary rocks dating back to between 136 and 65 million years ago. There are many interesting formations of columns, stalagmites and stalactites that have either a crystalline or a blood-red appearance. These deposits resulted from the continual dripping of mineral-rich water.

La Tigra (13)

This national park of 29 sq. miles (76 sq. km) includes the highest parts of the San Juancito Mountains, which are covered by humid tropical and subtropical forests. Up to 5,906 feet (1,800 m), the elevation is dominated by storax and pine trees. Above this elevation, a mountainous type of forest (cloud-forest) characterized by oaks, laurels and Clusias (epiphytic plants that are notorious tree-stranglers) represents the prevailing vegetation. Some of the more noteworthy animal species are several cats (margays, pumas, wildcats, and ocelots), collared peccaries, and quetzal birds.

EL SALVADOR

Montecristo (14)

This national park of 7.7 sq. miles (20 sq. km) is located at elevations between 5,250 and 7,940 feet (1,600 and 2,420 m) near the border with Guatemala. Several peaks lend variety to the landscape: Cerro Brujo at 7,021 feet (2,140 m), Cerro Miramundo at 7,855 feet (2,394 m), and Cerro Montecristo at 7,933 feet (2,418 m). The most characteristic feature of this area is the forest cover, which is the last piece that has been somewhat preserved in the region. At higher elevations, the forests of pines and oaks change to forests of different species of oaks and laurel trees, with epiphytic orchids, lichens, and ferns. The park is the last refuge for many animal species that have disappeared elsewhere. Among the inhabitants of the park are howler monkeys and black-handed spider monkeys, white-lipped peccaries, white-tailed deer, brocket deer, pumas, cacomistles, and spotted skunks. Birds include quetzals, bar-tailed trogons, several types of hummingbirds, and birds of prey.

NICARAGUA

Saslaya (15)

This national park covering 45 sq. miles (118 sq. km) is located in the department of Zelaya, between 656 and 5,250 feet (200 and 1,600 m) of elevation. Within its territory, ancient volcanoes, like Cerro Saslaya 5,230 feet (1,594 m), dominate the landscape. The area is covered by a rain forest, which becomes a cloud forest at higher altitudes. The park is crossed by the Rio Wani, many of whose tributaries have small waterfalls. The animals are particularly interesting here, with spider monkeys, howler monkeys, capuchin monkeys, giant anteaters, ocelots, jaguars, white-lipped peccaries, Baird's tapirs, and white-tailed deer all inhabiting the park. Some of the birds include tinamous, quetzals, keel-billed toucans, and several types of Amazon and macaw parrots.

This national park of 21 sq. miles (55 sq. km) is only 12 miles (20 km) away from Managua. Of the three volcano craters in the park, one is still active. The park borders on the Pacific Ocean at the Masaya lagoon. The dry climate allows the growth of a dry tropical forest and a savanna. Because they have been hunted, the number of vertebrate animals in the park has decreased. Recently, however, there have been signs of a revival of the populations.

Mesaya Volcano (16)

COSTA RICA

Santa Rosa (17)

This national park of 81 square miles (210 sq. km) is located on the Pacific coast in the northern part of the country. It is bordered on the east by the Pan-American Highway. A large part of the protected zone consists of the so-called Murcielago area. About 40 percent of the park is flat, the rest being small hills. Along the shore there are wide, saline beaches. The vegetation can be divided into three characteristic zones—mangrove swamps, savanna, and forest. The forests consist mostly of deciduous trees which lose their leaves every year growing along rivers or in marshy zones. The animal populations are making a comeback since the establishment of the park. The wide variety of animals includes mammals such as white-lipped and collared peccaries, black-handed spider monkeys, jaguars, margay cats and other carnivores, collared anteaters, and white-tailed deer. There are numerous interesting species of birds, and in the estuaries, turtles come onto the beach to lay their eggs, often creating interesting sights. Almost 300,000 of these turtles were observed in only one year's time. The park has picnic areas and trails that are furnished with biological information.

Cabo Blanco (18)

This national reserve of 4.5 miles (12 sq. km) is located at the tip of Puntarenes Peninsula. It extends from sea level to an elevation of 1,165 feet (355 m) on sedimentary rocks that were formed in the Miocene epoch. The most characteristic feature of the reserve is the island of Cabo Blanco, almost 1 mile (1.5 km) from the continent. The rocky coast has many cavities and caves whose walls are covered with guano, a substance composed chiefly of the dung of sea-birds and bats. Capuchin and spider monkeys, Baird's tapirs, jaguars, ocelots, and other cats inhabit the park. A large colony of frigate birds nests along the coast.

Santa Rosa (19)

This small island group is located about 5 miles (8 km) from Puntarenes Port. These islands serve as a refuge for colonies of seabirds like frigate birds, brown pelicans, brown boobies, and snakebirds. There is also a notable coral reef near the island of Negritos.

Poas (20)

This park of 15 sq. miles (40 sq. km) located 37 miles (60 km) from San Jose has a volcano by the same name. The volcano rises from an elevation of 5,250 feet (1,600 m) to a peak of 8,885 feet (2,708 m). The Poas Volcano has five craters, one of which is still active. The last important period of eruption ended in 1954. The humid forests become cloud forests at higher elevations, and they typify the vegetation of the area. These forests are dominated by various species of oak trees as well as by many species of epiphytes. Some of the most easily seen animals are the native mountain squirrels, deer, Baird's tapirs, collared peccaries, jaguars, and quetzal birds.

Braulio Carrillo (21)

This national park which is 124 sq. miles (320 sq. km) is located in the central plateau, extending between 1,640 and 9,515 feet (500 and 2,900 m) of elevation. The landscape is composed of canyons and steep valleys, dominated by two inactive volcanoes. About 95 percent of the rain forest in this humid climate is primary growth. The makeup of the large variety of forest species changes according to altitude. Capuchin monkeys, black-handed spider monkeys, mantled howler monkeys, Baird's tapirs, and brocket deer live in the forest. Notable birds include quetzal and Montezuma oropendolas.

Tortuguero (22)

This national park comprising 72 square miles (189 sq. km) is located on the Atlantic coast in the state of Limon in an extremely humid and hot zone. The annual precipitation is approximately 197 inches (5,000 mm), and the average annual temperature is 77°F (25°C). Rock formations originated from flood plains in the Quaternary period, two to three million years ago, although rocks formed by more recent volcanic activity are also found here. Many canals cross the predominant rain forest, creating marshy zones.

In this photograph, straw has been placed in a tree to dry. This is one of the traditional practices of the local farmers. Primitive techniques and customs still survive in the Central American countries, especially in the zones having a more strictly agricultural economy. These traditional practices have not caused particular damage to the habitats of the plants and animals in these areas.

110

The most common aquatic plant is the water hyacinth. This is the favorite food of the manatee, the most interesting animal of the park. Other notable species of mammals include kinkajous, jaguars, pumas, ocelots, and giant anteaters. Macaw parrots, king vultures, cormorants, and snakebirds also make their homes in this area.

Various species of sea turtles come onto the beach to lay eggs. The large-scaled *Atractosteus tropicus* fish is found in the waters of this park. Many species of crabs, including land crabs and the ghost crabs, can be seen along the shores.

Chirripo (23)

This national park of 165 sq. miles (430 sq. km) is located in the southern part of the Cordillera de Talamanca, between 4,000 and 11,500 feet (1,200 and 3,500 m) of elevation. It is dominated by the highest mountain of Costa Rica, which culminates in the peak called Chirripo. The dark rocks of this peak are granite-textured and crystalline. Glacial lakes and other glacial structures are found at an elevation of about 11,155 feet (3,400 m). There is a mountainous type of rain forest that grows in areas not exceeding 10,925 feet (3,330 m) in elevation. Beyond this tree line lies a plain called a "paramo." The park is home to a large variety of animals including Baird's tapirs, jaguars, pumas, brocket deer, and Brazilian cottontail rabbits. The notable birds include quetzal, volcano juncos, red-tailed hawks, hummingbirds, and barred parakeets. A few interesting types of salamanders are found here as well.

Cocos (24)

This national park of 12 sq. miles (32 sq. km) is located about 310 miles (500 km) from the continental coast and 390 miles (630 km) from the Galápagos Islands. It includes the islands of Cocos, which are of volcanic origin and are covered by a type of premountain rain forest vegetation. On the shore there are coconut palms, cherimoya trees, and *Erythrina fusca*.

There are many native animals on these islands, including the anole lizard (Townsend's false chameleon), the Cocos Island finch, and fourteen species of ground finches. Shorebirds include the magnificent frigate bird and the great frigate bird.

Corcovado (25)

This national park of 161 sq. miles (418 sq. km) includes the Osa Peninsula (Puntarenas province) on the Pacific coast, and the small forest-covered island of Cano. The elevated areas consist of volcanic rocks and sedimentary rocks formed in the Cretaceous period between 163 and 65 million years ago. The coastal lowlands were formed by flood plain deposits in the Quaternary period.

Several types of vegetation patterns are present. These include forests with a wide variety of species, lowland forests with 165-foot-tall (50 m) trees forming galleries, lagoons and forests with poor drainage, swampy zones with a predominance of Raphia trees, and estuaries with mangrove trees. Coconut palms and hibiscus grow in the areas bordering the beaches.

This luxuriant vegetation is an ideal environment for many species of animals. There are 139 species of mammals, 285 species of birds, 116 species of amphibians and reptiles, 16 species of freshwater fish, and a large variety of invertebrate animals, including swallowtail and brush-footed butterflies. The most wide-spread mammals of the park are Baird's tapirs, collared peccaries, deer, jaguars, ocelots, margay cats, wildcats, giant anteaters, black-handed spider monkeys, and squirrel monkeys. Interesting birds of the park include harpy eagles and goat-billed herons. Significant reptiles of the area are American crocodiles and caimans. At least four species of sea turtles lay eggs here.

La Amistad (26)

This large protected area covering 1,737 sq. miles (4,500 sq. km) is located between Panama and Costa Rica in the Cordillera de Talamanca, between 656 and 11,650 feet (200 and 3,550 m) of elevation. The landscape is characterized by mountain peaks, valleys, streams, lakes, and waterfalls. There is a great variety in vegetation, ranging from humid tropical rain forest to cloud forest to alpine grassland (paramo). The terrain is covered by a mountainous rain forest with oaks, many mosses and liverworts, ferns, bromeliads, orchids, and other epiphytes. At about 9,840 feet (3,000 m), one encounters areas of grassland and humid zones with high altitude plants. The park is home to a wide variety of animal species, including tapirs, quetzals, and green and black pit viper snakes.

PANAMA

Baru (27)

This national park of 55 sq. miles (143 sq. km) is located 9 miles (15 km) from the border of Costa Rica. It is positioned at high elevations in the Talamanca Mountain chain, which includes the Baru Volcano—the highest peak of the Panamanian territory. There are two main types of vegetation in the park. They are humid tropical forest of the foothills and the mountains.

Both types of forest have many kinds of epiphytic plants growing on trees, creating spectacular effects. However, meadows are also found in the area, and one can also see a subalpine tropical type of grassland. The quetzals, great curassows, collared peccaries, coatis, pumas, and brocket deer are among the most interesting species of animals.

Barro Colorado (28)

This artificial island is considered a national monument, and it is the highest point of the country at an elevation of 560 feet (171 m). The protected area covers 20 sq. miles (52 sq. km), with a central nucleus of 6 sq. miles (16 sq. km). The vegetation is the same as that found in Sobernaia Park (below).

Various species of animals inhabit the park. Some of these animals have been introduced into the island (e.g., the black-handed spider monkey). Some of the other animals include the ocelot, the margay cat, the wildcat, the otter, the cotton-head marmoset monkey, and the howler monkey. There are also numerous species of birds.

Sobernaia (29)

This national park of about 85 sq. miles (220 sq. km) is 1.25 miles (2 km) from the island of Barro Colorado. The area is covered by a lowland rain forest in which there are zones of secondary forest that have seventy-year-old trees. This park is important because of the large number of plants (over 1,500 species) and for the extraordinary population of birds (560 species).

Altos de Campana (30)

This national park is 18 miles square (48 sq. km). It is located on the Pacific coast, and it ranges over very steep terrain. It has volcanic and intrusive rocks and an abundance of water. The average temperature is 69° to 71°F (21° to 22°C). The annual precipitation is about 105 inches (2,700 mm).

Except for a small cultivated area, the protected area is covered by luxuriant primary and secondary forests of the humid tropical premountain and mountain types.

There are two species of marsupial animals (the woolly opossum and the common opossum), vampire bats, collared peccaries, and brocket deer. In addition, approximately 175 species of birds have been counted in the park.

Darien (31)

This large national park has an area of 2,304 sq. miles (5,970 sq. km). It is located in the province of Darien in Panama on the Panama-Colombia border. Its elevation ranges from sea level to 4,920 feet (1,500 m). The natives farm about 10 percent of the area. The park is crossed by the Chucunaque and Tuira rivers, which flow into the Pacific Ocean. The ocean tides move up the end sections of these rivers for a few miles. The coastal landscape is a complex mosaic of beaches, rocky sections, and saltwater and freshwater swamps.

Botanists believe that the Darien ecosystem is the most varied in all of tropical America. It ranges from coastal mangrove swamps to areas of cuipo trees and cloud forests in the highest zones. The animal species include bush dogs, giant anteaters, capybaras (the largest living rodent), ocelots, spider monkeys, Baird's tapirs, and harpy eagles. Caimans and American crocodiles are found in the coastal areas.

DUTCH LESSER ANTILLES

Curacao: Christoffel (32)

This national park of 5.7 sq. miles (15 sq. km) is located in the northern part of the island of Curacao, extending to an elevation of 1,230 feet (375 m). Its sedimentary soils have been modified by the movement of the earth's crust. The vegetation is composed of prickly pear cacti, columnar and globular cacti, acacias, and other plants. In several zones there are species of fig and evergreen trees, as well as four species of orchids.

Some of the animals that are found here are white-tailed deer, cottontail rabbits, white-tailed hawks, crested quail, conure parrots, snakes, iguanas and other lizards, and native species of land mollusks (snails).

Bonaire: Washington-Slagbaai (33)

This national park is located in the northern part of the island of Bonaire, and it extends from the coast to an elevation of 709 feet (241 m). It has an area of about 22 sq. miles (59 sq. km). The average temperature is 80°F (27°C). There are some native plant species, such as the *Curacao opuntia*-cacti. Other plants include columnar cacti, acacias, and other species of opuntia cacti.

Among the birds of the park are some Amazon parrots and native conure parrots. There are several species of lizards and iguanas and about thirty species of land mollusks (snails and slugs). Along the coasts there are mangrove swamps and coral reefs.

Following pages: Shown is a view of a bay of the island of St. John. Even in the West Indies there are only a few areas that have not been disturbed by the presence of people. The activities of humans have greatly modified the original environments of the islands.